THIRD EDITION

SCENERY
for Model Railroads, Dioramas & Miniatures

Robert Schleicher

4/99 Genfund 23⁰⁰

Published by

krause publications

700 E. State Street • Iola, WI 54990-0001
Telephone: 715/445-2214

Please call or write for our free catalog.
Our toll-free number to place an order or obtain a free catalog is 800-258-0929
or please use our regular business telephone 715-445-2214
for editorial comment and further information.

Library of Congress Catalog Card Number: 98-87370
ISBN: 0-87341-709-7

Printed in the United States of America

Contents

CHAPTER 1
Scenery and Dioramas

Fig. 1-1. The effect of the Slim Gauge Guild's HO scale scenery is spectacular, but its methods are so simple that anyone can follow them.

The model builder is often considered more a technician than an artist. And this is true if you are simply snapping together a plastic-model car kit or running a toy train around a plugged-together track. But once you paint the model or add even a simple structure or two to a toy train, you are entering the realm of the artist. In fact, *anyone* who re-creates scenery in miniature is an artist. The sim-

ple act of duplicating or, in the case of some architectural models, *suggest*ing scenery is as much of an art form as painting with pastels or oils. Creating a three-dimensional scene, such as a diorama or model railroad, combines the artistic skills of the sculptor and the painter. The ultimate development of the modeler-as-artist, of course, is embodied in the dioramas in museums, particularly in science and industry museums. These scenes were created by professional modelers, but you do not have to be a professional to create a scene of artistic value.

The techniques used to re-create nature and its effects in three-dimensional miniatures have been so refined and simplified over the years that anyone with the skill to snap together a plastic kit can create a realistic scene. If you apply the lessons in this book to any scene, you will have produced a work of art.

Architectural and Topographic Models

Most of the techniques in this book go one step beyond building architectural models, since the purpose of most architectural models is to provide a conceptual image of the terrain and landscaping that will complement a proposed structure. It is easier to envision the entire scene from these models than from a plan or isometric drawing. But even the model is often a relatively simple version of the final scene. The subtle effects of shading and weathering that are added to a military diorama or model railroad scene are not needed on architectural models.

The architectural model can take several forms, ranging from a rough outline of the structure itself to a complete scene that includes the structure, the surrounding terrain, trees and shrubs, and often people and vehicles. When the architectural model includes the surrounding terrain as well as the structure, it is called a topographic model. The topographic designation applies when the scope of the model includes more terrain than structure. For example, a complete housing or industrial development, where structures occupy only a fraction of the available acreage, are topographic.

The amount of detail on a landscaping model and, in fact, its actual scale can vary considerably. Some landscaping models for housing or industrial developments are built to a scale as small as 1/100 to show the number and position of trees, streets, sidewalks, and grassy areas. Other landscaping models might be built to a scale as large as the 1/24 scale model in Figure 1-3. The most common architectural modeling scales are shown in Figure 1-4.

Dioramas

The creation of a model aircraft, military tank, or model railroad locomotive used to be a complete project in itself. We could use our imaginations to envision how the model appeared in real life. Today, most modelers go beyond the model itself and create a diorama—the model as well as its environment or historical context. Since nearly every model is part of a historical scene (or, in some cas-

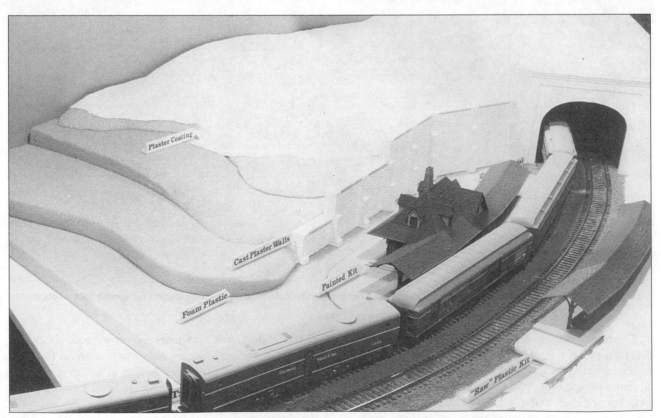

Fig. 1-2. For featherweight scenery, shape contour profiles in polyfoam insulating board, as was done in this scene made by the Pittsburgh HO scale Modular Club.

Fig. 1-3. AMSI's professional modelers created this 1/24 scale landscaping model using the firm's ground foam, fiber, and tree truck kits.

Scale	Other Designations for the Same Scale	Common Uses	Scale	Other Designations for the Same Scale	Common Uses
1/220	Z	trains	1/48	O(¼"=1')	trains, aircraft, and military models
1/160	N	trains			
1/100	—	architectural models	1/40	—	architectural models
1/87	HO	trains	1/35	—	military models
1/80	—	architectural models	1/32	⅜"=1'	architectural models, aircraft,
			1/29	—	car, trains, and ship models
1/76	British: OO scale (4mm=1')	military models and trains	1/25	—	model cars
1/72	1"=6'	military and ship models	1/24	½"=1'	architectural models, model cars, trains and dollhouses
1/64	S (³⁄₁₆"=1')	architectural models and trains	1/16	¾"=1'	architectural models
1/60	—	architectural models	1/12	1"=1'	dollhouses and architectural models
1/50	—	architectural models	1/10	—	architectural models
			1/8	1 ½"=1'	architectural models
			1/1	full-scale (12"=1')	movie, TV, and theater sets and props

Fig. 1-4. Model-scale proportions.

es, a scene from the future or from a fantasy world), the techniques developed by professional model makers to create those scenes are precisely the ones the amateur modeler should follow. Weathering a model airplane so that it looks just as it does in flight is one form of diorama. However, if you are modeling a military tank, a race car, a steam locomotive, or a Victorian house, the model will almost always have a missing part; the scenery supplies that missing part. Some modelers even feel that a model military tank, race car, or Victorian house is just a toy until it is placed in its natural setting.

For most modelers, the constraints of time and space demand that only a few models be placed in dioramas. The model railroader can complete not only a railroad station but also the station platform, parking lot, and other surrounding details. This station diorama can exist on its own on a bookshelf until the model railroad itself is ready for the station scene. Then the station as well as the surroundings can be arranged and set in place.

Scenery Made Simple: The Reference Cards

The scenery-made-simple techniques here are designed to allow anyone to complete an artistically perfect scene, including subtle texture and shading effects, in as little time as possible. At the end of this book you will find twenty-six Reference Cards that provide virtually all the information you need to create any scene in this book. For easy reference, tear out the cards, punch three holes in the left hand side, and insert them into a three-ring binder. You can protect the pages with clear acetate sleeves made especially for use in three-ring binders. These reference cards will be handy when you truly are in the hands-on phase of building scenery. The formulas on the Reference Cards use water-soluble materials wherever possible, so you can usually proceed through the entire process in just a single evening without having to wait for one step to dry. The materials noted contain the lowest amount of toxic substances and have the least odor.

Some of the suggestions, such as the extensive use of ground foam for texture and artist's matte medium for cement, rather than dyed sawdust for texture and white glue, are more costly than their alternatives. In every instance, however, the lower-cost alternative is not as realistic, or it has some other fault. For example, white glue can crack, whereas matte medium is flexible. Near-equal choices of materials will be noted, such as deciding whether to search for a realistic tree trunk rather than purchasing Woodland Scenics or AMSI cast-metal trunks. In these examples, the commercial product noted produces results equal to natural growth, and they also

can save countless hours of searching. Don't be intimidated by the "Do's and Don'ts" (Reference Card 2). Do follow the charts. Only examples of the Do techniques have been selected for this book. *Don't* examples can be found in nearly every issue of every hobby magazine. There are exceptions to these rules. If you are an accomplished artist, you may be able to paint a backdrop that is as effective as those sold by HO West! or Detail Associates, or the photomurals from Vollmer or Faller. You may even have developed a technique to tease sawdust so that it looks like grass. The purpose of the Don'ts charts is to point out some techniques you may have read about but haven't tried—techniques that are too smelly, toxic, time-consuming, or unrealistic, or a combination of any of these undesirable qualities. This book offers you the experiences of more than a dozen professional architectural modelers and diorama builders and skilled amateurs, as well as *effective* commercial products. These methods are not only the most realistic, but they are nearly failure proof because they have been proven.

Building a Basic Diorama

The best way to learn any new skill is to dive right in with both hands. You can build a simple 1 x 1-foot-square diorama on a single ceiling tile or scrap of plywood for little cost and learn much about scenery building in the process. The diorama can be even smaller than a foot square if you simply want to create a small scene for 54mm (approximately 1/32 scale) military miniatures. The larger diorama will be adequate for displaying a piece of armor (Figure 1-5), a barge-loading coaling trestle (Figures 1-6 and 1-7), or a racing-garage scene (Figure 1-8). The completed diorama can be glued to the back of a custom-made picture frame (see Figure 1-5) for display on a bookshelf, or it can be included eventually in a complete model railroad.

Keep your first diorama as simple as possible. For the diorama in Figure 1-5, George DeWolfe used a flat piece of plywood covered with Celluclay, artist's matte medium, and gravel for the basic scenery. The basic diorama for these two scenes is only a slightly higher pile of Celluclay with a greater variety in rock and rubble size.

Planning the Scene

The artistic effect in George DeWolfe's prize winning dioramas is no accident. George has been a professional artist and photographer, and photography in particular showed him the importance of balance and composition. George follows six simple rules to ensure that his dioramas are realistic recreations:

Fig. 1-5. A painted and weathered Testors/Italeri 1/35 scale Panzer I tank is the focal point of George De-Wolfe's military diorama.

Fig. 1-6. This turn-of-the-century coaling dock won a prize for Irv Schultz in an NMRA national contest.

1. Each diorama is like a frame from a cartoon or a TV storyboard. It implies action and captures a fleeting moment.

2. There is enough world around each figure or vehicle to imply continuation beyond the scene.

3. None of the elements of the diorama, not even the cobblestone road, are parallel to the edge or frame of the scene.

4. The major point of emphasis in each scene is shifted slightly away from the center to give balance to the rest of the scene.

5. Each diorama is composed so that the viewer's eye is led from one element to the next. This allows the entire scene to be appreciated.

6. The weathering on the figures and vehicles is blended into the ground colors so that the entire scene becomes a world in itself.

Building from the Ground Up

The dioramas in this chapter incorporate techniques from nearly every other chapter. Start the simplest diorama by mixing about a half-cup of Celluclay (or American

Fig. 1-7. The coaling dock diorama later became an integral part of Irv Schultz's HO scale model railroad.

Fig. 1-8. Parts from a half-dozen 1/25 scale plastic car kits and some strips and sheets of balsa wood were used for Tom Reed's diorama.

Art Clay papier mâché) with water, as indicated on the side of the package. Because Celluclay and American Art Clay papier mâché products contain extra binders and cements, they are much better than the traditional newspaper-and-wallpaper-paste papier mâché formula. They can be spread as thin as 1/16 inch over as much as a 12 x 12-inch-square surface without cracking. However, the surface must be supported on a picture frame or base so that it will not flex and cause the papier mâché to crack. The material can also be built up to an inch or so thick for small hills or lumps in a roadway. For elevations of more than 1/4 inch, wadded-up wet newspapers are best.

If you are going to run a railroad track across the diorama, use the cork roadbed to elevate the track and to simulate the ballast shoulders. (If you are building it at an oblique angle, remember Rule 3.) The cork roadbed can be used to simulate elevated highways, with several strips placed parallel to one another. Don't cover the cork with Celluclay or papier mâché for a railroad right-of-way, but do cover it to simulate dirt or paved roads. You'll find all the information that you need on roads and roadbeds in Chapter 3.

If you are going to use any large rocks or other details, such as a piece of bombed-out wall, push them into the Celluclay or American Art Clay papier mâché while it is still wet. When the material dries, it will approximate rough scale-model earth. You can color it with Polly Scale earth colors (see Chapter 6) and sprinkle on some loose, sifted dirt before adding vehicles and figures.

Fig. 1-9. Celluclay can be spread into a thin layer to provide texture and uneven ground shapes.

A basic earth-colored diorama can be the starting point for an endless array of fine details. Several layers of sifted dirt held in place with water and artist's matte medium can produce a rutted road. Before you add the vehicles and figures, read every chapter and pick one element from each to include on this practice diorama. You can add rock castings, weeds, trees, puddles of water, and even ice and snow. The close-up detailing possibilities are endless. You could even add empty cans and other debris. This diorama is also the place to practice weathering and people-painting techniques. If you make a mess, scrape off what you can, cover it with another layer of papier mâché or Celluclay, and start over.

A Piece of the Whole

Irv Schultz is a master at creating dioramas that later become part of his permanent model railroad layout. The barge-loading coal dock in Figure 1-6 is shown as it was when entered in the diorama division of a National Model Railroad Association contest. Figure 1-7 shows it nestled into Irv's model railroad. Complete model railroad scenes can be planned into your existing railroad, or you can plan some future railroad to include several scenes you have built over the years and had no space for.

Don't let the diorama format discourage you from using several track elevations and other multilevel scenes. It is relatively easy to plan a model railroad to fit minor differences in the elevations of sidings. Be sure to keep an accurate record of all color and texture formulas you use so that you can match old scenery to new.

Modular Model Rairoads: The Ultimate Diorama

The practical limit on the size of a single diorama is about 24 x 24 inches. Anything larger is usually too heavy for a bookcase or shelf. If you have 24 x 48 inches of available space, however, why not consider making a portion of a complete model railroad—a module. A module is either a section of a larger model railroad or just large enough to incorporate as many as a half-dozen individual diorama scenes. The modular model railroading concept is simple: You build a 2 x 4-foot section of the railroad with the extreme ends matched to the extreme ends of hundreds of other 2 x 4-foot sections. Because of the interfacing ends, any one module can be connected to another to create a model railroad two feet wide and as long as there are modules. It is also possible to construct a few buildings on 6 x 6- or 6 x 12-inch boards and incorporate them into a module.

Several N, HO, and O scale modular standards exist, and there are literally thousands of modules. Most major cities have a modular model railroad club that meets about once a month to assemble a layout with the members' modules. David Smith's HO scale desert scene (Figure 1-10) is an example of one module that was connected to others. The club supplies the 4 x 4-foot corner modules, so the resulting layout is O-shaped with space for the operators inside the O and spectator areas around the outside.

Modules and dioramas have one feature in common: They provide enough space in a *small* space for some real model railroading—from buildings to scenery to train-switching operations.

Fig. 1-10. David Smith used bent pipe cleaners, MLR cactus, and ground foam to simulate the sparse Arizona desert vegetation in HO scale.

Module Standards

Today, few of us have the space at home to devote to a permanent model railroad. Fewer homes have basements or attics and there's seldom room in the garage. Many model railroaders are now building heir layouts as one or two 2 x 4- or 2 x 6-foot modules that can fit in a den or spare bedroom.

These layout modules are built to standard to match other modules so that a dozen or more modelers can connect (interface) their modules together in a random order to build a complete model railroad. The system allows the modeler to operate a layout that, typically, may be as large as 30 x 90 feet, built from as many as 100 different modules. But the individual modeler needs to only build a house and a single 2 x 4-foot module.

The most widely accepted standards for modules are for N scale. NTRAK publishes standards that have been used to build more than 1,000 modules all over the world. Clubs get together in shopping malls in cities and at national conventions to assemble layouts that range in size from about 16 x 30 feet to 200 x 300 feet!

The NTRAK 16-page manual of specifications for the standard module is just $1 and a 100-page "How-To" book on building and troubleshooting N scale modules is $9. Order either from NTRAK, 1150 Wine Country Pl., Templeton, CA 93465.

There are also hundreds of 2 x 4- and 2 x 6-foot modules like the Midwest Mod-U-Trak and Midwest Valley modules shown in the color section. Unfortunately, there are no national standards for HO scale modules. If you want to build an HO scale module, find a nearby club that is already creating modular layouts and follow their standards. If you simply want to build a module, use the NTRAK standards. Similar modules have been built using S scale, O scale and even 1/24 scale model railroad models.

CHAPTER 2
Imitating Nature

One of the major mistakes that modelers make is to try to duplicate someone else's model, rather than nature. Although it may seem easier to match the scenery of another modeler, the opposite is true: The *best* you can hope for is a caricature of the model. This book offers you all the techniques you need to duplicate the scenery of the professional diorama builders and gifted amateurs. What you will not find here, of course, is nature itself. For that, you must go directly to the source.

The research involved in finding the scene for your diorama (or a variety of scenes for your model railroad) can be fun in itself, and it will increase your appreciation of the world around you at the same time. The best way to begin is to combine vacations and weekend trips with your hobby. A second way is to search for color photographs of the scene you have in mind. Before you set out

on your quest, you should have some idea of the scene you want to duplicate. For example, if you are modeling the Rio Grande narrow gauge in Colorado's Rocky Mountains, try to plan a vacation there. A trip to the Sierra Nevadas won't help. This is another reason why it's a mistake to copy a model: You have no way of knowing whether the modeler actually researched the scenery. If you cannot visit the area you want to model, try to find calendars, back issues of magazines like *National Geographic,* or large illustrated books such as those series published by Time-Life or the "on sale" illustrated books in large bookstores.

The paints, dyes, textures, and shapes are included here, but for their specific applications, you must do some research. Before you go into the real world, arm yourself with the *model* half of your project. Buy Floquil Polly Scale, and

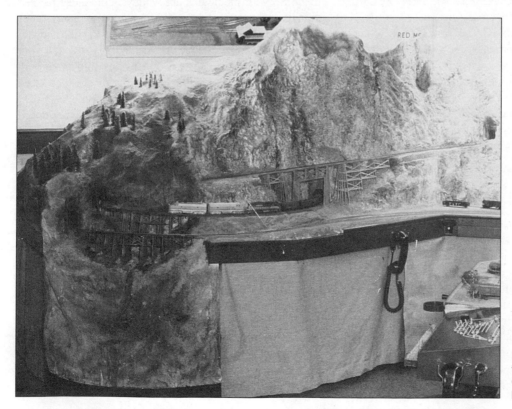

Fig 2-1. Lee Nicholas created the floor-to-ceiling scenery on his HO scale railroad from photographs.

Sher-win Williams color charts (Reference Card 8), or those of other paint brands, so that you can match the colors of nature. Buy a complete assortment of ground polyurethane foam greens and yellows too, and take everything with you on your field trip. Also take a camera and a notebook to record where you took each picture and which paint and ground foam colors most closely match the scene. You will have to take some artistic license here, of course. The colors in nature may be more intense or more faded than the color chip and ground foam samples. But you can correct for that when you paint the model, or you can alter the amount of light that falls on it.

Natural Lighting and Color Matching

To match colors to nature, match the color chips and ground foam textures to your color photographs. To bring the *effect* of nature's lighting indoors to your miniature scenery, you will have to make major color corrections. You will discover, for instance, that the color chips and ground foam samples do not match the colors in your photographs. Remember that you matched the color samples outside, as they appeared in sunlight, and that the developing process alters the color values of photos to some extent. Your color prints and pictures in books and magazines will help you determine what color the dirt really should be on your indoor scenery. And the notations you make when you match the color chips and ground foam to nature will help because most will likely be only a shade or two away from the closest match.

Do not try to match an actual rock or leaf to the color chips. Closeup color is seldom the same as the color of the entire tree or the color of rocks on a cliff. The color effect you need for a model is that seen from a greater distance. Fortunately, the reduced size of the scene in photographs is similar to the scale of your model. The highlights and shadows that will result from rock casting, earth texture, and ground foam will also provide the variations in shadow and highlight.

The Shape of Nature

Your research into the nature of nature will help you duplicate the illusive shape of the hillsides and foliage in the real world. The photographs will tell you two important things: what the major shape of the hillsides and trees should be, and how rough the shapes should be. For example, are the hills steep like the peaks of the Rocky Mountains, or are they gentle like the hills of Kansas? (A 45-degree slope is steep in nature.) Are the surfaces of the slopes rough like the exposed rock faces of the Rocky Mountains, or are they smooth like the grass-covered hills of Kentucky's Blue Grass area? The plaster or foam-

plastic scenery will have to be shaped to match the degree of the slopes on your model. The rough texture of the hills can be duplicated with one of a variety of patterns for latex rubber rock molds (see Chapter 4).

Before you try to duplicate tree shapes, you will want to know whether to buy or build a trunk structure that will re-create, for example, the columnar shape of a cypress tree or the mushroom shape of an oak. The tree's texture can be smooth and carefully pruned or rough like an ancient pine. Both textures, and everything in between, can be duplicated with ground foam (see Chapter 7), but you must know the natural effect in order to duplicate it. Similar research will provide the data you need for weeds, roads, water, and all the other details that make the Rockies so much different from Kentucky's rolling hills.

Planning in Three Dimensions

One of the most common uses for scenery is to make a tabletop model railroad more realistic. Unfortunately, too many model railroaders confuse *the sequence* of the railroad in relation to scenery. It is difficult to create credible scenery as an afterthought to the model railroad. The construction of the scenery should begin at the same time as the construction of the railroad—at the planning stage. For example, if you lay the track before you plan your embankment for a trestle, you will have to do a lot of bracing and build a lot of benchwork to provide a place for the embankment. So your mountains and valleys, cuts and fills, and tunnels and trestles should all be planned with at least as much precision as is used in laying the track. Hills and valleys, though, are more three dimensional than track. If your mind does not translate two dimensions into three with ease, and few do, follow the lead of the most experienced model railroaders and build a model of your model.

Dr. Joseph Nicholls is one of the most experienced model railroaders around. The National Model Railroad Association has awarded him a well-earned Master Model Railroader certificate of achievement. Dr. Nicholls knew that he had designed a complex model railroad, and he wanted to be certain that the tracks were separated enough to allow for a 45-degree-or-less slope along embankments between lower- and upper-level tracks. He drew a track plan of 1-1/2 inches to the foot (where 1/8 inch equals 1 inch) so that he could duplicate structures with blocks of painted balsa. This model is a topographic or architectural model like those described in Chapter 1. Dr. Nicholls went so far as to cut small chunks of fine-pore sponge to represent the trees. His model took more than many of us spend on our actual railroads, but it accomplished the goal more quickly than trying to adjust the track locations and scenery contours on the full-size HO scale layout. He discovered, just from the section of the

Fig 2-2. Dr. Joseph Nicholls made this 1/8 inch: 1-foot model of his proposed HO scale layout to ensure successful scenery.

model shown in Figure 2-2, that the embankment in the upper left of the photograph was too steep: He solved the problem by reducing the uphill grade to lower the upper-level track.

Models and Mock-Ups

Sometimes you might want to make full-scale mock-ups of your proposed buildings or scenic features. The hill-building techniques in Chapter 4 allow you to shape all the basic contours with wadded-up, wet newspapers. Similar see-how-it-looks-before-you-build techniques can be used for model structures.

Robert Schlachter, who specializes in narrow-gauge prototypes, is one of the most skillful modelers in the United States. One of his projects is a modular model railroad depicting a two-foot, narrow-gauge railroad of his own creation, but it is based on the Maine railroads of the 1920s. The shelf-style railroad leaves little room, particularly in O (1/4) scale, for the relatively large structures of a Maine seaside town. To be sure that his buildings would fit, he assembled cardboard mock-ups as shown in Figure 2-3. The passenger station, with its hexagonal bay and peaked roof, and the group of houses were modified several times to achieve the desired effect. Now the thin cardboard mock-ups can be used as patterns for the sheet

Fig. 2-3. The shapes to the left of this O scale scene will later become buildings on Robert Schlachter's layout.

styrene or basswood walls of the actual models. The same technique could of course be used to modify kit-built structures by making full-size duplicates on a photocopy machine or by tracing the wall outlines with a pencil onto cardboard. The kits then could be cut down to provide a balanced grouping.

Geology for Modelers

Some experienced model railroaders claim that you need a college course in geology in order to create a realistic model. Nonsense. Instead, you need to develop the eye of the landscape artist and learn to observe the real world. For example: One of the better scenery builders discovered that the shape of broken coal was more like the shape of scale-model rock than most real rock. Like many modelers, he uses latex rubber to make flexible molds of broken coal for precolored plaster rock castings (see Chapter 4). This is the same type of skill that led modelers to discover that sagebrush twigs were almost exact scale-model tree trunks (see Chapter 7). For the modeler, actual observation of the lay of the land is more important than a geology course.

Of course, you should have a basic understanding of how nature operates so that you can avoid the most glaring mistakes in re-creating scenery in miniature. Mountains were formed as the earth's plates shifted and folded. Aside from earthquakes and a few active volcanoes, most of the earth's surface has been shaped by glaciers and by erosion caused by wind and water. To the modeler, nature offers relatively few cliffs: Most of the mountains and hills look like those in Figure 2-4 on at least three of their sides. The cliffs in most areas appear only on one side of the hill or mountain where the land has faulted. The exceptions are the buttes associated with the southwestern desert and canyons formed by rivers.

Too many modelers concentrate on the cliff faces and ignore the more common gentle faces of hills and mountains. This is because they try to duplicate the efforts of other modelers, or because they did not plan their scene from the beginning and now lack adequate space.

The views in Figure 2-5 are the four most common hillside cuts. These cuts may eventually become tunnels if the walls become too high. There is no simple rule for determining whether a cut is deep enough, with the hilltop high enough above the tracks, to justify a tunnel. If the banks leading to the tunnel are steep, you will need less mountain over the tunnel. If the track cuts through earthen banks with slopes of about 30 to 45 degrees, the cut must be very deep indeed before a tunnel is necessary. Only exposed rock slopes are steeper than 45 degrees. A tunnel through soft substances such as dirt, loose rock, or sandstone is always lined with wood or stones (Figure 2-6). The cutaways in Figure 2-5 reveal some of the essential elements that are missing from many model railroads. The two most important features of any railroad cut are the drainage ditches on either side of the track.

Tunnels

The two tunnels in Figure 2-6 show how the relatively shallow tunnels so common on model railroads can be made more realistic. There is little cover over either of these tunnels because both go through rock rather than dirt. The important element here is that most of the mountain is *implied* as sloping up and away from the tunnel. if you must have short and shallow tunnels, make sure to include more of the mountain. The wall can be located to the left or the right of either tunnel in Figure 2-6. The edge of the table also can be located far to the right or left. Model railroaders tend to slope all mountains upward

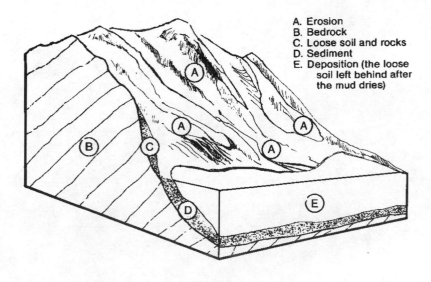

A. Erosion
B. Bedrock
C. Loose soil and rocks
D. Sediment
E. Deposition (the loose soil left behind after the mud dries)

Fig. 2-4. A cutaway view of rock and dirt erosion from mountaintops and slopes.

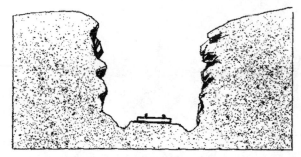

1. A near-vertical excavated embankment with a slope of 45° to 90°.

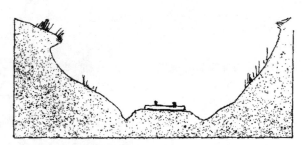

2. Overhanging embankment of clay and rock with slopes of 30° to 45°.

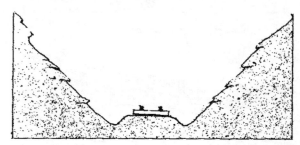

3. An exposed limestone and shale embankment with a 30° to 45° slope, usually covered with loose dirt and rocks.

4. The most common embankment, with slopes of 0° to 30°, usually covered with weeds.

Fig. 2-5. Four cutaway views of the type of terrain that creates different degrees of slopes in fills or cuts on either side of the track and drainage ditches.

from the edge of the table, but you can achieve more realism by allowing some to slope up toward the aisle. Make sure, though, that any slopes between the tracks and the backdrop (except for the earthen fills or embankments made by the railroad) slope upward toward the backdrop. This will give the viewer's eye a natural path to follow toward the horizon.

Simulated Rocks

A background in geology is no more important to the model railroader than a background in chemistry is important to the amateur chef. And in the case of model scenery, knowing too much can actually be a disadvantage. For example, the actual color of any rock is not what you want to capture: What you want to re-create in miniature is the entire *effect of* a rocky cliff or the whole meadow or a complete tree. Matching color samples to actual leaves or blades of grass or rocks produces a toy-like effect. If you expect your scenery to look real, you must try to duplicate a particular geographic area. The

name of the rock, whether sandstone or granite, is not important. What you want to know about the rock is its color and texture and, beyond that, the shape of the hills on the tops and sides of the rocky cliffs.

Prepare a list to guide you in your search for natural materials. And take some color photographs along the way. Look for real rocks, pieces of broken coal, and even well-weathered driftwood that duplicate the texture (not necessarily the overall shape) of the rocky cliffs and cuts you want to model. Also look for weeds to use as trees or bushes and dirt to use as real dirt. The slopes and crests of hills can be formed with wadded-up newspapers to match the angles and shapes in your photographs. Start your list of natural items now, but read the other chapters for many of the other natural items you will need for a realistic diorama. Figure 2-7 shows four items that duplicate the surfaces of real rocks in exact scale. The lesson here is that textures suitable for model rocks do not necessarily come from *actual* rocks. If you cannot locate the type of rocks you need for your cliff faces, go to a rock or gem shop (these shops also have petrified wood) or look at different types of hard and soft coal.

Typical granite cliffs. Tunnel may have no linings or portals.

Fig. 2-6. Modelers often place tunnels through the center of mountains. Instead, place tunnels through the shoulders of rock cliffs.

On limestone, sandstone, or shale cliffs, tunnels require wood, stone, or concrete linings and portals.

Fig. 2-7. Master patterns of real rocks for latex rubber molds. *Left to right:* **granite, petrified wood, coal, and lava (foreground).**

18

In Chapter 4 you will find out how to use rocks or coal as patterns for latex rubber molds, which in turn will be used to make precolored plaster castings of the rocks. It also will show how to obtain the textural realism of real rocks or real coal. Never use real rocks to simulate rocks. They're far too heavy, their textures are out of scale for any model, and the colors are not realistic. The realism of a real rock is almost always destroyed when it is placed next to a scale-model human or animal figure.

Access Hatches for Model Railroads

Modern planning techniques for model railroads require benchwork that runs around the walls, with an occasional peninsula jutting into any available space in the center of the room. This system allows the operators and spectators to get closer to the trains. The benchwork is relatively narrow so that the modeler can reach the backdrop, and it allows the layout to be placed much higher than the older island-style layouts so that the horizon is closer to eye level, as described in Chapter 10. The higher the layout is placed, however, the narrower the shelf or peninsula must be; most of us can reach only about two feet without bending at the waist. One of the reasons for a conventional table-height model railroad was to provide access: most of us can reach more than three feet if we can bend at the waist. The most realistic way to display your models is to elevate them to at least chest level, about 48 to 54 inches from the floor.

For some track plans, the only way to maintain that 24-inch maximum reach and keep the models high enough for proper viewing (and to allow for an eye-level horizon) is to provide a few access hatches in the center of the layout (Figure 2-8). Access hatches can be disguised with the edges of cliffs, or they can be placed behind the crests of mountains. The same scenic profile that hides the access hole usually hides the tracks behind it. The types of access holes that need the special scenic treatments in this chapter are those used strictly for emergency track repairs or for rerailing trains.

Planning for Access

It is not fun to have to crawl under a model railroad to reach an access hatch. And the task becomes formidable when you cannot even squeeze your shoulders through the hole. Access holes must be a minimum of 18 x 24 inches for most of us, and perhaps wider if you are broad shouldered. To be able to turn your body comfortably, 24 x 24 inches is even better. You will disguise the access hole in any case, so the extra few inches usually won't make much difference. Obviously, you don't want to place an access hole where a track can cross it; if your layout lacks even an 18 x 24-inch space, you have crammed in too many tracks.

The principle of a lift-out access hole is the same as the lift-out access panels into most attics; a support frame is built around the *underside* of the access hole and a piece of plywood is dropped in from the top. To open the hole, you simply push up the plywood and move it aside. If you are disguising the edges of the access hatch with the

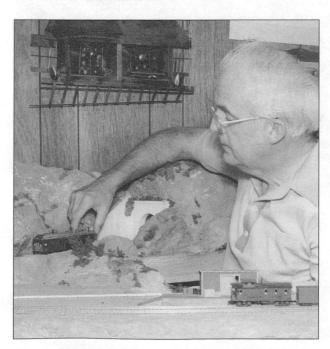

Fig. 2-8. The 24 x 24-inch access hole in Willard Jones' HO scale railroad allows him to reach derailed locomotives easily.

Fig. 2-9. A lake covers Willard Jones' 24 x 24-inch access hole. The straight edges are disguised by fallen trees, a road, a dam, and coarse-ground foam.

shores of a lake (Figure 2-10) or a river (Figure 2-11), the access hatch must be removable by dropping it down. The construction of the access hole, then, requires a frame of 1 x 2 boards around the underside of the hole, so when you plan for a 24 x 24-inch opening, make the actual opening a few inches larger. If you're crammed for every inch, a simple diagonal support across each corner is fine. You won't touch the inside corners of the access hole when you move in or out of it, so the cut off corners should not be a problem.

Camouflaging the Access Hatch

After you have completed the benchwork for your layout and the surrounding frame, supporting frame, and plywood cover for the access hatch (some layouts require more than one access area), pay particular attention to how the surrounding scenery will meet the edges of the hatch. The obvious solution is to camouflage the access hatch with a lake, which is what Willard Jones did in Figures 2-8 and 2-9. It is also possible to make only the water portion of the lake removable. You will have to hinge the corner braces so that you can drop the access hole (and the lake) downward to remove it. With

this technique, use a coping saw or a saber saw to cut the shoreline of the lake into the plywood access hatch cover. Buy a piece of frosted pebbled window glass the size of the access hatch, and build a detailed lake *bottom* into the opening in the plywood. Then cover the lake with the glass. Install the hatch and lake and build the upper scenery so that it matches the lake bottom and shoreline, like the glass lake on the Sverna Park Model Railroad Club layout in Figure 2-10 (also shown in the color section). When you remove the lake, the shoreline remains, so the details along the shore must be fairly robust to withstand accidental buffeting.

You can also camouflage the access hatch with a river shoreline, following the same technique, if you can locate the access hatch or the river so that a big river bend coincides with one or two edges of the access hatch. A dam across the river could camouflage another edge of the hatch, or you could place a highway or dirt-road bridge across the river to coincide with an edge of the access hatch. The river bend and another side of the access hatch could also disappear behind a small hill.

The same suggestions for a river apply to using a paved road as the boundary for an access hatch. Figure 2-11 shows in cross section how the edge of a river must

Fig. 2-10. A frosted-glass lake, such as this one on the Sverna Park Model Railroad Club layout, can drop downward to reveal a hidden access hole.

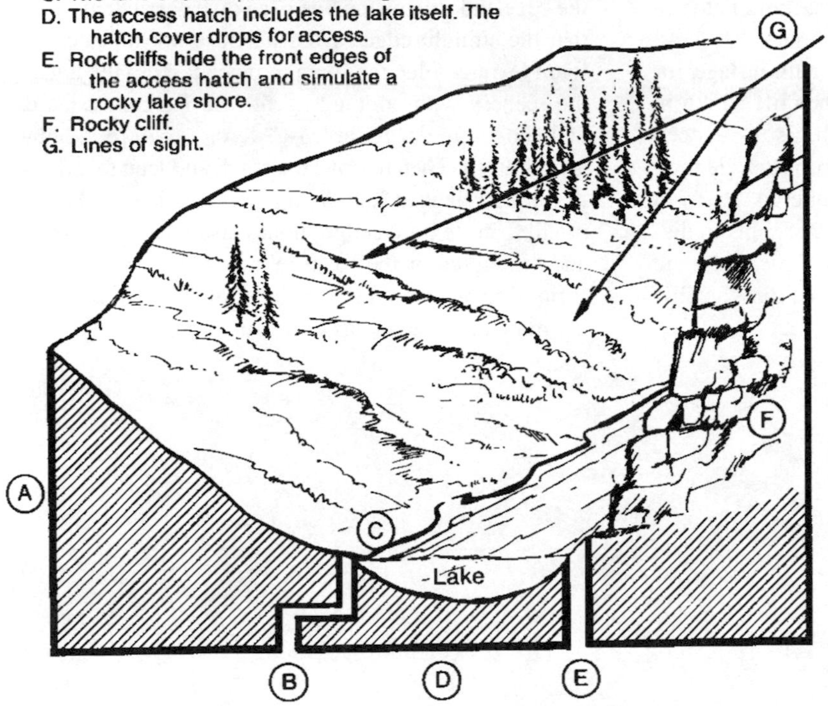

A. Rear (backdrop).
B. A step in the hatch provides alignment of scenery edges.
C. The lake shore hides the rear edge of the access hatch.
D. The access hatch includes the lake itself. The hatch cover drops for access.
E. Rock cliffs hide the front edges of the access hatch and simulate a rocky lake shore.
F. Rocky cliff.
G. Lines of sight.
A
B
C
D
E
F
G
Lake

Fig. 2-11. The viewer's line of sight across any access hatch determines the technique used to disguise its edges and cover.

SOUTHERN PACIFIC
SAFEWAY

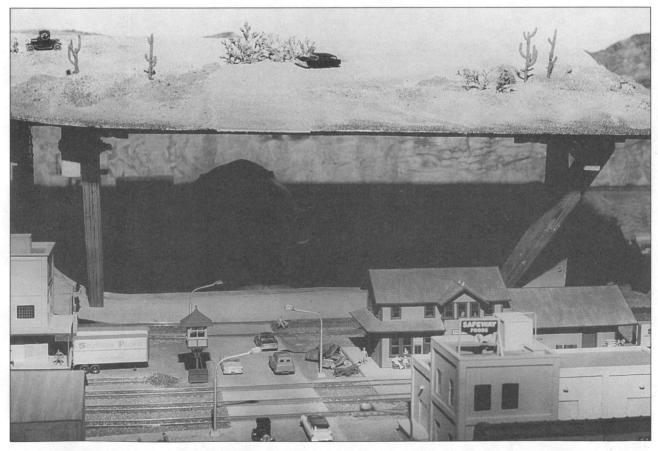

Fig. 2-12. The desert-covered access hatch on LeRoy Thompson's HO scale layout has hinged 2 x 2 boards to support the hatch cover.

be shaped through the scenery and benchwork so that the access hatch can drop downward. LeRoy Thompson used the edge of a road and the ballasted back edge of a track to disguise the edges of his lift-up access hatch in Figure 2-12.

A vertical rock cliff is an excellent camouflage for one or two edges of any access hole if the cliff's bottom edge, where it joins the access hatch, is just steep enough so that the joint is not visible from the viewing aisle. Most of the downsloping cliff can be visible from the aisle so just the last vertical inch or so seems to disappear over the edges. A few matching rocks on the hatch itself will help carry on the deception that the cliff continues.

Perhaps the most effective camouflage even for the most obvious edge of an access hatch is ground foam in medium and coarse grinds. Simply sprinkle the foam along the edge and expand the line to a wave or patched design so that the straight edge of the hatch is not repeated in the foam texture. Glue the foam in place to both the hatch and the scenery with bonding agent (see Reference Card 12) and allow it to dry for at least two days before moving the access hatch. Then remove the hatch and let it tear the foam in a rough, jagged line. When you replace the hatch, the rough foam-textured edge should disappear in the shadows and highlights of the foam. You may have to add just a sprinkling of foam in some places along the edge (and apply more bonding agent) if the joint is still visible.

CHAPTER 3

Railroad Rights-of-Way, Streets, and Roads

The focal point of most model railroad scenery is the track itself, and not just the rails and ties, but the twenty-scale feet or so on either side of the track known as the right-of-way. This stretch of land is deeded to the railroad and maintained by it. The right-of-way extends beyond the ballast and includes bridges, culverts, earthen fills that lead to bridges, or cuts that lead to tunnels. Model railroaders, always cramped for space, often cram so much scenery into their limited space that they ignore the railroad right-of-way, the most important scenic element of all.

Ballast and Borrow Pits

The term *borrow pit* is commonly associated with highway construction. The borrow pit is the ditch beside many state highways that was left when the dirt to elevate the highway itself was "borrowed" from the land. Nearly all full-size railroad mainlines-including the quaint two-foot narrow gauge railroads in Maine, the three-footers in Colorado, and the shortlines such as the Sierra Railway and the Ma & Pa—have both ballast and borrow pits. The railroads usually called borrow pits "drainage ditches," and these ditches are as important a part of railroad tracks as the ties or ballast.

The dimensions in Figure 3-2 provide an adequate-width right-of-way for standard or narrow-gauge model railroads. Most narrow-gauge railroads and branchlines

and even standard-gauge mainlines built before about 1905 did not have the luxury of the embankment shoulder (C in Figure 3-2). The ballast would tumble down the sides of the embankment on these types of rights-of-way. This lack of control over the position of the ballast shoulder (B) was what prompted the railroads to add additional ballast to the embankments to produce the shoulder in (C).

The four tracks in Figure 3-2 show the differences between mainline and branchline trackage and ballast, embankments, and drainage ditches. The reasons for the difference in the construction of the surfaces beneath the tracks were twofold: cost and the need for heavy- or light-duty roadbeds to match the intended traffic. A spur track to an industry that ships relatively light materials doesn't have to be as strong as one that supports 100-car unit trains of 100-ton loads per car seven times a day. The width and style of roadbed construction also varied with the period; one of the most amazing aspects of the Union Pacific's abandoned roadbed near Promontory, Utah, which dates back to about 1870, is its extremely narrow width—barely wider than the ends of the ties.

The four types of roadbeds in Figure 3-2 can be used to help define the type of railroad you want to duplicate in miniature. It would be unusual, for example, to have seen a Shay-type logging locomotive working along well-ballasted and drained track like that on the far right. And it would have been impossible for a Union Pacific Big Boy steam locomotive to operate over either of the

Fig. 3-1. Mike Bishop's N scale right-of-way has fresh ballast on the main line, old ballast on the siding, and two sets of power lines.

A. Width of ballast at tie level in scale feet:
  Standard gauge (4' 8½''): 9 feet
  Narrow gauge, 3-foot: 7 feet
  Narrow gauge, 2-foot: 6 feet

B. Width of ballast shoulder in scale feet:
  Standard gauge (4' 8½''): 15-16 feet
  Narrow gauge, 3-foot: 9 feet
  Narrow gauge, 2-foot: 8 feet

C. Embankment shoulder: Width 20-24 feet. Used only on mainline standard gauge since about 1910.

a. Dirt ballast is used for industrial siding or light-duty branchlines.
b. Rock ballast was used on mainlines and branchlines from about 1850 to 1900.
c. Rock ballast and elevated ballast slopes were used on mainlines from about 1900 to 1950. Note drainage ditches on either side.
d. Since 1940, mainlines have been placed on elevated earth-and-pebble fill with elevated ballast slopes. Note drainage ditches on either side.
e. Dirt road with 6 x 6 wood planks at flangeways.
f. Wooden crossing.
g. Metal or bolted wooden crossing.
h. Highway bridge beneath railroad.

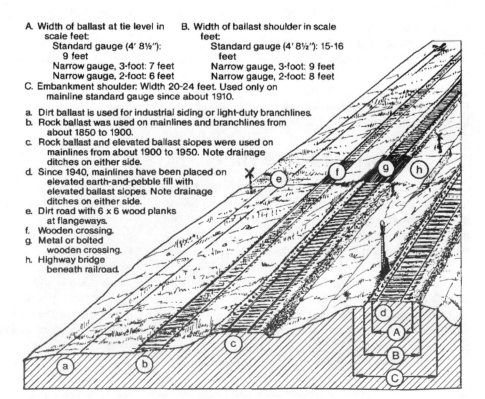

Fig. 3-2. A cross section of a railroad right-of-way shows the different shapes and sizes of roadbeds and crossings.

Fig. 3-3. Ed Patrone has begun to texture his scenery (right); the open-grid benchwork is still visible on the left.

tracks on the left. If your model railroad includes mainline, older sidings, branchlines, and industrial tracks, you might want to duplicate all four kinds of roadbeds on your layout.

Modeling the Right-of-Way

To provide a place for drainage ditches and for potential fills and valleys, elevate the roadbed and the subroadbed supports for the tracks at least three inches above the framework for the benchwork. If you use egg-crate or open-grid benchwork (Figure 3-3, left), elevating the track-work is a simple task. The tabletop should be cut

away so that the edges of the right-of-way extend only as far as they would on the real railroad. Use the widths in Figure 3-2 as a guide. The subroadbed and roadbed for a narrow-gauge railroad or a turn-of-the-century standard-gauge line would need to be only about two-thirds as wide as those for a modern railroad.

Once you have built the subroadbed, roadbed, track, and ties (ballast can be installed *after the sce*nery), you can proceed with cuts, fills, or tunnels.

Planning for Bridges and Trestles

With open-grid construction, you can actually complete most of the scenery work before installing bridges. Steve Hatch used open-grid construction for the HO scale layout in Figure 3-4, with a 1/4-inch plywood subbase, 1/8-inch Upsom board (a cardboard-like wallboard sold through lumber dealers), and hand-spiked rails on wooden ties. He completed the basic scenery shape and textures and installed wood supports that later would be covered with sheet plastic bricks and stones to simulate the bridge abutments. The bridge on the middle-level curve has been started by replacing the plywood and Upsom board over the span with longer wooden bridge ties and the wood supports that will later become the deck of a wooden trestle. The actual trestle bents will be cut to fit the distance from the bottom of the deck to the surface of the scenery. The long upper curve will be spanned with a long trestle to connect two wood truss bridges—one over the now-dry riverbed and the other over the middle- and lower-level tracks. The upper-level track has not yet been laid. The technique used to pre-

Fig. 3-4. Steve Hatch shaped and textured the scenery before adding the bridges and trestles on his HO scale railroad.

pare the layout for bridges can also be used with the lightweight extruded-polyfoam scenery-construction method in Chapter 5 (and shown in the color section).

Albert Hetzel used the more common method of installing model bridges: He lifted the portion of track for the bridge and attached it to the bridge itself. Only the bare wood backings for the bridge abutments are in place (Figure 3-5). The actual scenery shape beneath the bridge has not been installed yet. The track extends beyond the length of the bridge to leave space on each end for the guardrails that railroads use inside of each track's running rails to prevent derailed stock from jumping the track and falling off the bridge.

The precise alignment of the rails in every direction is as critical at bridges as at other rail joins. Actually, it's risky to use Steve Hatch's approach of completing the scenery before installing the bridges. But the risk is min-

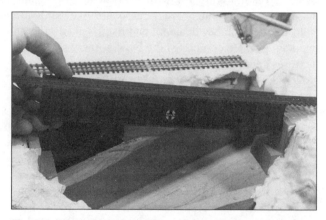

Fig. 3-5. Albert Hetzel completed this deck-girder bridge and its track before finishing the scenery that will go below the bridge. The bridge is a Campbell kit.

imized if you use the portion of track to be removed for the bridge as the pattern for the track that will rest on the bridge itself. Extend the rails (or the rails and ties if you are using plastic ties on ready-laid track) at least two inches beyond the ends of the bridge, as Albert Hetzel did. By using the shell-style scenery-shaping technique, with Hydrocal plaster and paper towels, it's relatively easy to break or cut through the plaster to install bridge abutments or to provide wooden supports for the bottoms of trestle bents.

Ed Patrone's HO scale layout is an extension of the basic diorama theory. Ed's layout is larger than average—filling a 14 x 15-foot room (see Figures 3-3 and 3-6)—but he has planned it carefully, spending the extra time to make the scenery as important as the railroad. The tracks, for example, are located so that there is enough space for realistic hill slopes of 45 degrees or less between the upper and lower tracks.

Ed's planning also included the location of bridges, those over tracks and those that would span later highways or roads and streams or rivers. It would be difficult to add a 4-foot-long replica of a wooden trestle (Figure 3-6) to any model railroad if the trestle was not part of the plan. Ed not only planned for the trestle, but he actually built the trestle first with wooden supports for the bases of the end trestle bents. He did not, however, glue the trestle to the bents; he removed the trestle, leaving the wooden supports for all the bases of the trestle bents. The plaster-and-paper-towel scenery was then installed *around* each bent's wooden support to leave the exposed wooden top of each bent clear to ensure the proper fit with the base of the trestle. The scenery was painted and textured and the trestle was replaced, but each bent was held in place only

Fig. 3-6. This 4-foot-long wooden trestle rests on a 1/2-inch plywood riverbed on Ed Patrone's HO scale layout.

with a thin bead of rubber cement so that the trestle could be removed again if the layout was dismantled or altered. Finally, loose sifted dirt and ground foam were dusted around the tops of the wooden supports for the trestle bents to bury the bottom of the bent and the exposed supporting board.

The center twenty or so bents are all the same height, so they simply rested on a flat piece of 1/2-inch plywood that was firmly attached to the benchwork. Again, the actual places where the trestle bents were to touch the ply-

Fig. 3-7. A 1 x 4 scrap elevates the foot of the center bridge abutment on Sy Simonton's layout while the riverbed plaster is completed.

wood bottom of the ravine were covered with plaster, dirt, and texturing only after the completed trestle was in place with its rubber-cement mounting. When the scenery was complete, the lower portion of the trestle was painted with a wash of about 20 parts water and 1 part Polly Scale paint to match the color of the scenery. This coat blended the trestle into the scenery and gave it a weathered look of splashed mud and windborne dust.

Tunnels

The interior walls and the portals of tunnels must be installed *before* the mountains that cover them are constructed. Sy Simonton's O scale wooden tunnel portals and interior were assembled with an open top so that he could reach over the walls and into the top of the hollow mountain to rerail cars or locomotives (Figure 3-8). He also installed small lights on either end of the tunnel for inspecting the track inside in the case of derailments. Similar construction techniques can be used for the interior walls of brick or stone tunnels. For tunnels cut through rock, place a wrinkled aluminum-foil mold over the tracks and shape it with wadded-up-newspapers. Cover the foil with a layer of Hydrocal-soaked paper towels, then apply two additional layers. When the plaster sets, remove the newspapers and foil and paint the interior. For inside larger mountains and hence longer tunnels, the interior can be made removable by simply resting it over the track that will go inside. If maintenance or derail problems occur, the plaster shell-style liner can easily be removed.

Fig. 3-8. Sy Simonton finished the inside of this wooden tunnel before he started the O scale mountain and cuts leading to it.

Streets and Roads

Streets and roads, like the railroad tracks and rivers, are the thread that leads viewers to feel that there is a link between the real world and the model. The street or road can lend a romantic atmosphere to a scene by winding out of sight behind a hill (or ending abruptly at the edge of the table or diorama) to suggest that real people come and go along it. Models of such vehicular paths are some of the most challenging aspects of scenery building because everyone *thinks* he knows exactly what a street or road looks like. Once again, refer to the real world or to color photographs when you re-create streets and roads.

Planning for Traffic

Few model railroaders have the foresight to include the path of a winding road when they plan mountain scenery. With few exceptions, the real railroads' rights-of-way are paralleled by roads or highways. Even the narrow-gauge railroads that challenged the Rocky Mountains and the Sierras were often located just a few dozen or a few hundred feet down the mountainside from the original stage or toll road into the wilderness (Figure 3-9).

A model railroad scene usually looks more credible with a road near the tracks than without one. But the scenery must be planned so that the cuts and fills for the roads are included in the space allocation for the scenery.

It is not necessary to support roads with the sturdy benchwork and subroadbed needed to support the tracks. The support for the roads can be made from corrugated cardboard supported by the same wadded-up newspapers that support the shapes of the mountains. However, you must prop sticks or other cardboard strips beneath the roads to be certain they are nearly level side to side. Take care with uphill grades for roads; they usually climb no more than twice as steeply as the railroad. There is no need to make roads as wide as they are in the real world; as shown in Chapter 9, the art of selective compression can be used to make a scale 16-foot-wide road pass as a replica of a real one that is 24 feet wide.

Dirt Roads

Dirt roads must be planned just as carefully as paved roads. You don't have to worry about dirt roads on level farmland, but there must be space for at least a scale 8-foot-wide level space from side to side for a dirt road

Fig. 3-9. The dirt road dominates this scene of the Slim Gauge Guild.

through mountainsides. Using real dirt on a dirt road is the most realistic medium. Dirt selection and preparation techniques in Chapter 6 give the finest possible grit for the road's surface.

Most dirt roads and virtually all paved roads have a borrow or drainage pit on either side of the road on both level ground and through any cuts. You can build up the road with a thin layer of plaster and scrape the surface of the still-wet plaster smooth with a scrap of 1 x 4 wood. Keep the road as level and smooth as possible. Scale-model ruts and ridges can be created with just a few extra granules of dirt. Use the soaking agent and bonding agent on Reference Cards 11 and 12 to hold the loose dirt in place. The only special technique that is needed to differentiate between plain dirt and a dirt road is evidence of traffic. You can build up a center ridge with a strip of dirt spread through the notch of a file card folded in half. Spread the pile of dirt down the center of the road with your fingertip. Allow the bonding agent to dry for at least a week, then scrub the road with a coarse typing eraser or a track-cleaning eraser such as a Bright Boy (Figure 3-10). The eraser will smooth out the road by moving it only in the direction of traffic, and it will lighten the color of the dirt slightly.

Railroad Crossings

With the exception of modern rubberized inserts, nearly all railroad crossings are either wooden planks placed between the rails or continuations of the concrete or blacktop pavement. The rubberized crossings can be simulated with pieces of plain plastic cut into scale-size 2 x 8-foot blocks and glued between the rails to the tops of the ties. The plastic must be thick enough to bring the roadway almost to the tops of the ties. To be safe, any model railroad crossing should be between .005 and .010 inches (the thickness of paper or a business card) *below the* tops of the ties so that coupler pins and gears cannot accidentally drag on the crossing. Use wood strips to simulate real wood crossings.

If you want superdetails for either type of crossing, buy some of the smallest nut-bolt-washer castings from a model railroad dealer (Grandt makes them in plastic) and cement them to the crossing to simulate exposed bolt heads. The rubberized modern crossings and the planks weather to a shade of dark gray. Touch the bolt heads with dabs of aluminum-colored paint where car tires wear them and Polly Scale Boxcar Red to simulate rust where tires do not travel across the crossing.

If you want to simulate a concrete or blacktop-paved crossing, buy some twine or rope at a hardware store or macrame from a craft store. The rope should be about the same size as the rail on your model track. Lay a piece of the twine or rope tightly against the inside edges of both rails (Figure 3-11). You can hold the twine in place with a straight pin or a scale railroad spike or two if necessary. Leave at least two inches of loose twine beyond the crossing to serve as a handle. You can now spread molding plaster or plaster of paris down the road and across the crossing to bury temporarily both the twine and the rails. Use a scrap of wood to scrape the still-wet plaster so that it is just barely below the tops of the rails. Let the plaster harden, then immediately and carefully pull out the twine to leave the flangeway clearances inside each rail. This same technique works especially well for duplicating trackwork laid in city streets.

Fig. 3-10. Real dirt is the best material for simulating dirt roads, but the road surfaces must be rubbed with a hard rubber eraser.

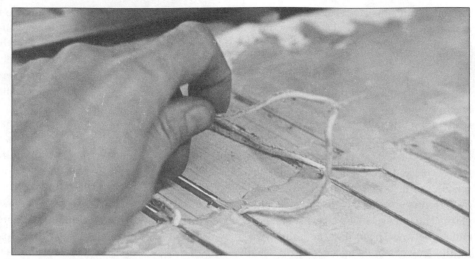

Fig. 3-11. Bury twine along the insides of the rails when shaping plaster roads, and remove the twine (as shown) after the plaster hardens.

Concrete and Blacktop Roads

Concrete and blacktop roads can be made in any scale from 1/220 to about 1/16. Blacktop roads are usually rougher, but the roughness should not be modeled in Celluclay or in any other rough texture. A three-inch-wide, flat-ended putty knife or spatula can be used to apply and spread the plaster. The plaster for roads should be mixed with more plaster than usual to yield a mixture that is just a bit softer than fresh bread dough or child's modeling clay. It is wise, too, to color the water before

mixing the plaster to give a medium-gray color to the dried road surface.

For city streets and other level paved areas, tack a curb of 1/16-inch-square stripwood to the edges of the road. Fill the area between the strips with plaster and use the tops of the strips as a straight, even guide for a block of wood to spread and level the top of the road. If the final surface is still rough, wrap some medium-grit sandpaper around a scrap of 2 x 4 lumber to make a sanding block, then sand the surface perfectly level. The wood strips can then be removed. If you are adding curbs, the

Fig. 3-12. Outline the cracks and seams in plaster/concrete roads and sidewalks with ink-filled knife cuts, as Tom Knapp did in this scene.

Fig. 3-13. The realism of this blacktop road is heightened with Country Trains decals and street signs.

strips can remain. For curbs, tack down slightly larger square strips of wood to provide the proper curb height for the scale of your model. Use curb-height strips (plus the 1/16-inch road thickness) for both the front and back edges of the curbs and repeat the road-building process to finish the curbs.

The only difference between a model of a concrete road and a model of a blacktop road should be color (see Reference Card 3). On country roads, however, the blacktop usually crumbles into the sand beside the road, leaving slightly wavy edges. You can duplicate this effect simply by slightly sanding the exposed edges of the plaster (and/or the 1/16 inch wood-edge strips) with coarse sandpaper. The dirt techniques in Chapter 6 apply to the edges of paved country roads as well.

Most concrete country roads are edged with several feet of blacktop and a sand shoulder, so the road edges for either concrete or blacktop are almost identical. Before you paint this kind of road, mask off the concrete with masking tape, using a ruler to guide your hand while finishing and painting the shoulders. Remove the tape and paint and stain the concrete.

Cracks in the Road

Concrete and blacktop roads crack with age and both are patched with beads of tar. Concrete roads, however, have additional perfectly straight cracks that are also filled with tar about every twenty feet or so. These straight tar seams are expansion joints that allow the concrete to expand and contract with a minimum of cracking.

Some sidewalks have similar lines, placed about every three feet, to provide a decorative effect that helps disguise the actual tarfilled expansion joints. You can simulate either type of crack on blacktop and concrete roads by slicing lightly into the surface with a sharp hobby knife. Use a steel ruler to guide the knife. With a paint brush, flow a trace of india ink into the cracks, and before the ink can dry, wipe away the excess with a tissue. Apply only about 6 inches of ink at a time so that you can wipe it away before it dries. The ink will remain *only* in the cracks. You can use a wash of 19 parts water to 1 part Polly Scale black paint to highlight the texture of concrete streets and curbs and a similar wash of lighter gray to weather blacktop streets. The fine sand that collects in the gutters, center, and edges of blacktop roads is easiest to simulate by spraying on a wash of gravel-colored Polly Scale with an airbrush. Simulate the similar effect of rubber tire wear on blacktop roads with a brushed-on wash of black along the traveled areas.

Street Markings and Signs

Scale Scenics and Noch make street signs and decals for on-the-street markings in HO scale. Since there is no standard size for such markings, they can also be used for N and O scale if the spacing of the letters is adjusted. This firm also makes decals for white and yellow lines. Several brands of model-airplane decals offer stripes that are the proper width center lines in any scale. When you apply the decals, use at least a dozen coatings of decal solvent, such as Micro-scale's Micro Sol, over the decal to force it to adhere to the rough plaster. Spray the decal-covered street with Testors DullCote to blend the decal into the street.

Ready-to-Lay Streets and Sidewalks

A number of firms, including Noch, Plastruct, Preiser, RR&F, and Timber Products make simulated blacktop roads sold in rolls or sheets for HO or N scale. The Preiser and Noch roads even include the white divider lines. The RR&F roads are gummy black material that can be spread a few fractions of an inch to fit tightly against the edges of tracks or to join two pieces. Plastruct sells its material in sheets in either black or a concrete gray. Plastruct sells

a similar texturing paint in the same colors. Any of these can be used as a substitute for the plaster roads described earlier in this chapter.

Details like guard rails and curbs are also available in HO scale. Pikestuff offers injection-molded plastic guard rails, simulated concrete parking barriers, and sidewalks. Preiser also offers curbs and guard rails. Some of the Heljan HO and N scale buildings include sidewalks and curbs. The techniques for making streets, described earlier, can be used to create plaster curbs and sidewalks which can be stained to represent rough concrete with cracks and tar strips.

Jim Providenza used a variety of natural growths for the limbs and trunks of these trees including Pride of madera, sagebrush and baby's breath. The twigs on most of the trees are fine wisps of Woodland Scenics Poly Fiber. The leaf textures are both fine-ground foam and flakes from K&S Scenery Products.

The experts at Architectural Scale Models assembled this 1/12 scale garden scene, complete with picnic, on a 24 x 24-inch framed piece of plywood. All foliage is crafted from AMSI ground foam-rubber material.

This lake is actually the roof of an emergency access hatch on the Severna Park (Maryland) Model Railroad Club HO scale layout. The water is frosted office-door glass with a wavy texture, used here to simulate the lake's surface.

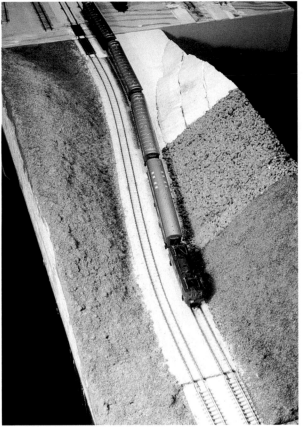

Paul Ingraham and Virginia Wilken built this N scale Interail module to demonstrate the use of Styrofoam insulating sheets. The Styrofoam is carved, contoured and stacked with white glue, then covered with plaster-soaked paper towels.

A stone quarry on Don Bozeman's NTRAK module. The rock cliffs to either side are cast in latex molds, but the seams where the rock has been quarried were carved with a knife, guided by a steel ruler.

This cross section shows the contours used on most mainline railroads. George Booth used industrial paper towels, dipped in Hydrocal plaster, to mold the embankment. Latex paint and Woodland Scenics' foam texture materials are used to create ground cover.

The Slim Gauge Guild's now-demolished HOn3 layout in Pasadena, Ca., included some of the most spectacular scenery ever created. The rocks were made of patching plaster, pre-colored a light gray and cast in latex molds. Scraps of plaster were then chipped and broken into rubble to create rock slides.

The O scale model railroad at the Buhl Planetarium in Pittsburgh is changed each year. This is the summer scene with the boats gliding through the real water in the river.

Real water flows over a navy blue metal "lake bottom" on the spectacular railroad in Pittsburgh's Buhl Planetarium and Institute of Popular Science. The trees and foliage are clumps of Yarrow weed, dyed and wired together to provide all the textures. Charles Bowdish and Herman Mike tear the 19 x 76-foot railroad apart and rebuild new scenes each fall.

The ocean is patching plaster, shaped by hand on Tom Knapp's N scale module. The wet look sheen is achieved by applying Artist's Gloss Medium after the acrylic color dries.

Ken Patterson and members of the Midwest Valley Modelers in Saint Louis created this winter scene. The horizon and distant trees are real because the module was moved outdoors in mid-winter while this photograph was taken. Baking soda is the best material to use to simulate snow. — *Ken Patterson photo*

Jim Miller used a variety of medium-size ground foam colors to create this farm on the Midwest Mod-U-Trak HO scale modular layout.

Steve Cryan used parts from junk plastic steam locomotives, Keil-Line castings and Chooch cast resin junk piles and gondola loads to create this scene near the locomotive roundhouse.

Harry Sage Jr. used some weeds for these Aspen tree trunks with Woodland Scenics Poly Fiber for the twigs. The leaves are the paper punchings left from the holes made by a Telex machine. Rit dye was used to color the leaves and they were attached with hair spray.

This 4 x 8-foot model railroad layout has a table built from a stack of three layers of 2-inch-thick Dow-Corning Styrofoam. The vertical edges of the Styrofoam are protected with 1/8-inch-thick cherry veneer plywood painted green. The legs are supported by 1/2-inch plywood triangles beneath each corner of the bottom of the stack of Styrofoam boards.

The stack of three 2-inch Styrofoam boards provides the depth needed to create the valleys that fall below the level of the tracks and roads. Here, the Styrofoam has been carved from beneath the tracks and roads with a hotwire cutter. The bridges will be installed after the scenic texturing is complete. The hills in the background were made with the "contour" method shown in Chapter 5.

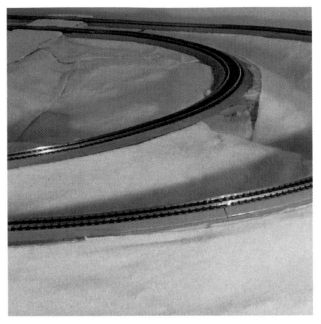

The "Grass-That-Grows" method of creating scenery textures begins with a layer of beige felt. Cut the felt to fit around the track and roadbed, but leave at least a 1/2 inch of excess felt. Glue the felt to the shaped scenery with latex-type contact cement and press the felt in place while the cement is still wet.

Use a craft knife to trim the beige felt so it is even with the edges of the ballast shoulders, the edges of any roads and the edges of any level building sites or parking lots. When the glue dries, tease the surface of the felt with a stiff wire brush like those used for cleaning machinist's files.

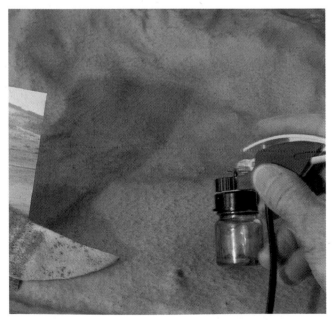

Referring to a photograph, use a shade of green acrylic paint to match the shade of grass you are modeling. I used a scrap of felt to test the colors. Mix the paint with an equal part water and spray it onto the felt to color just the already-teased fiber, leaving the underlayer of beige visible through the green.

Use a tea strainer to sift real dirt onto the felt. Use the wire brush, again, to work the dirt into the felt. When just enough dirt is applied, you will actually see (if you use a magnifying glass) the individual strands of green "grass" appear to be "growing" up out of the dirt. Trim the protruding fibers so none are longer than about 1/8 to 1/4 inch.

Simulate leafy weeds on the "Grass-That-Grows" felt and dirt surface with small clumps of ground foam.

Mix about 5 parts water to 1 part Artist's Matte Medium and spray the entire surface of the scenery with the mixture to bond all of the loose textures.

An HO scale workman standing almost knee-deep in a field of grass and weeds created with the "Grass-That-Grows" system.

Separate the individual tree trunk and limb forms from one another. The bulky shapes are dead leaves that must be plucked from the tree forms with tweezers. To straighten the tree forms, submerge them in a mixture of 10 parts Artist's Matte Medium and 1 part water, then hang the tree forms upside down with clothespins to dry and straighten.

The trees on the cover of this book were made using the Scandinavian weeds imported by Noch and Scenic Express. Both firms sell boxes of individual trees or you can buy the entire weed from Scenic Express.

Paint the trunk and lower limbs of the tree form dark gray to match the real tree you are modeling. Spray the upper twig portion of the tree with inexpensive unscented hairspray and sprinkle on fine-ground foam. Spray the foam with the hairspray and sprinkle on a second application of foam to produce a fuller and healthier-looking tree.

An alternate method of creating leaves on these tree forms is to use the flakes from Noch or K&S Scenery Products. Spray the tree with hairspray and sprinkle on the flakes to simulate leaves. A single application is usually enough with the flake-type simulated leaves. The tree is now ready for planting.

To simulate a thick forest quickly and inexpensively, cover the bulk of the area to be "forested" with Woodland Scenics Poly Fiber mesh. Pull the mesh apart to produce a lacy and see-through effect. Spray the Poly Fiber with hairspray and sprinkle on fine-ground foam to simulate leaves. Surround the Poly Fiber forest with two rows of the Noch or Scenic Express trees. Break off a few of the branches from these trees with tweezers and insert them into the top of the Poly Fiber to produce the effect that the trees beneath have the same form as the trees around the edges of the forest.

The Noch tree forms can be treated with fine-ground foam in browns and yellows to simulate a fall forest like this on a Walthers diorama. The conveyor leading to the Flood Loader Coal mine is visible to the left.

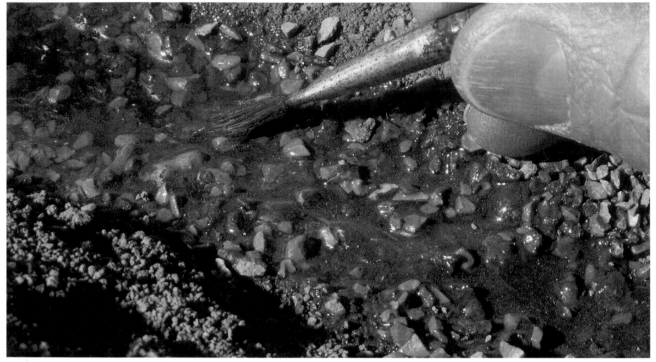

Simulate ripples and white water by "dry-brushing" wavy streaks of white over the surface of the water. To dry-brush, dip just the tip of the brush into the paint and brush a scrap of paper until just a trace of paint remains on the brush bristles, then apply that paint to the water.

The white water rapids on Bill and Wayne Reid's N scale Cumberland Valley model railroad were made with several layers of epoxy. The white water is paint dry-brushed over the epoxy, then covered with a final thin layer of epoxy to provide a "wet" look.

Norm Neilson used both AMSI and Woodland Scenics tree and hedge forms and ground foam scenery products to make the landscaped yard for this 1/12 scale dollhouse.

This vast expanse of water, perhaps an estuary of one of the Great Lakes or the edge of a large river, was made by dappling texture paint onto a sheet of plywood to create the waves, then painting the dried paste a dark green. The wet look was produced by a final coat of Varathane clear varnish. — *Ken Patterson photo, courtesy Wm. K. Walthers*

Dave Darcy used torn-apart plastic scouring pads and shaved balsa wood trunks to make the majority of the pine trees on his HO scale diorama. The pads were textured with several colors of fine-ground foam from Woodland Scenics. The bushes in the foreground are Woodland Scenics Poly Fiber treated with more fine-ground foam.

CHAPTER 4

Mountains, Valleys, Rocks, and Cliffs

Nearly every individual scenic feature for dioramas is available ready-built or as a simple kit. The textures and trees described in Chapters 6 and 7 are all available ready-to-use. Firms like Preiser, Plastruct, and Faller even make sheets of plastic that can be used virtually as-is to produce lakes, swamps, and marshes. When it comes to creating complete hillsides, mountains, and valleys, however, the Styrofoam or expanded-polystyrene one-piece hills and tunnels from firms like Bachmann and Life-Like are strictly for toy trains. This chapter, then, discusses the one area of scenery that you must do yourself. The thin-shell scenery technique, using Hydrocal plaster and industrial-grade paper towels, is just about as simple and easy a method as you'll find. Industrial-grade paper towels are available through janitorial supply firms and industrial drug companies. Buy them in brown or off-white—not blue.

For movable or modular model railroads and larger dioramas, conventional thin-shell Hydrocal plaster scenery can be too heavy for easy transport. Chapter 5, Lightweight Scenery, describes the proven alternative techniques for creating mountains, valleys, cliffs, and rocks with the least possible weight. One of those techniques utilizes Woodland Scenics Lightweight Hydrocal and industrial-grade paper towels, exactly as described in this chapter. By simply changing the basic scenery material from conventional Hydrocal plaster to Woodland Scenics Lightweight Hydrocal, you can use all the techniques in this chapter to create lightweight scenery.

One of the alternative techniques for lightweight scenery utilizes plaster-soaked gauze that is applied over wadded-up newspapers in virtually the same sequence as the Hydrocal-soaked paper towels described in this chapter. That technique, too, uses all the techniques in this chapter. The Hydrocal-soaked gauze produces the most lightweight scenery of all the plaster techniques because the gauze provides more strength than paper towels. It's the same material used to make casts to hold broken bones while they heal. Hobby shops carry the lowest-cost, plaster-soaked gauze like Woodland Scenics Plaster Cloth or Activa's Rigid Wrap.

Before you begin construction of any scenery you may want to read Chapter 5 to help you decide whether or not to incorporate the various lightweight scenery-building techniques. You should also decide if you want to utilize pre-cast, thin-shell lightweight rock casting technique, as described in Chapter 5, for the lightest possible weight of the finished scenery.

Reference Card 4 lists the most important tools and containers that you will need. You may have many of these on hand already, but purchase some extra ones since the chemicals used for scenery could contaminate them.

Paper and Plaster Scenery

The thin-shell scenery technique illustrated later in the chapter is recommended for several reasons, including simplicity, potential light weight, and relatively low cost. It also allows you a preview of the completed scenery before you mix any plaster. The thin-shell scenery shapes are made from industrial-grade paper towels (household paper towels tear too easily when soaked in wet plaster) and the brand of plaster called Hydrocal. Hydrocal was designed for making sturdy castings that would be nearly as hard as rock when dry; the material, in fact, is similar to alabaster when it dries. Any lumberyard can order Hydrocal for you. Hobby dealers sometimes stock Hydrocal or Woodland Scenics' Lightweight Hydrocal. The paper towels are soaked in a cream-consistency mixture of Hydrocal and draped over the scenery shapes to form all the

A. Loose ground foam and
   sifted dirt will hide the
   seam when the layout is
   reassembled.
B. Scenery, plaster, and track
   is cut between the plywood
   contour boards with a
   saber saw.
C. Thin-shell self-supporting
   precolored plaster scenery
   base made from Hydrocal
   and paper towels.

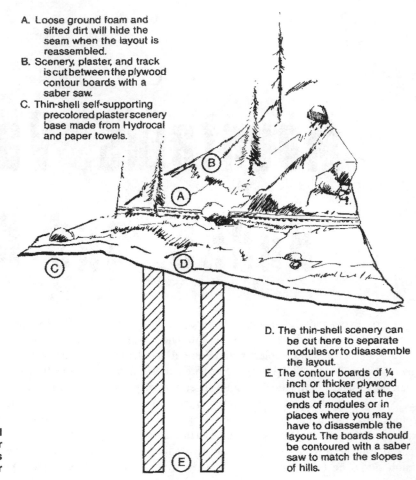

D. The thin-shell scenery can
   be cut here to separate
   modules or to disassemble
   the layout.
E. The contour boards of ¼
   inch or thicker plywood
   must be located at the
   ends of modules or in
   places where you may
   have to disassemble the
   layout. The boards should
   be contoured with a saber
   saw to match the slopes
   of hills.

Fig. 4-1. A cutaway section of thin-shell
scenery. The two cutaway plywood contour
boards (E) are needed only if the layout is
cut to make it movable or for use as modular
layout sections.

scenery surfaces. The Hydrocal-soaked paper towels are strong enough to be self-supporting after the plaster sets if two or three layers are used. But the actual shapes of the mountains and valleys must be built up with another material before applying the Hydrocal-soaked towels or Hydrocal-soaked gauze. You could use the traditional wire-screen-and-board approach to shaping the scenery, but there is no need for such substantial supports. Wadded-up newspapers provide ample support for the towels until the plaster sets. The newspapers can then be removed.

Newspaper Mock-Ups of Full-Size Scenery

The interesting advantage of using the thin-shell scenery technique is that the supports for the mountains and valleys are actually full-size mock-ups. The mock-ups must remain in place until the Hydrocal sets. If you don't like the shape of the scenery, you can change it before you apply the Hydrocal-soaked paper towels or gauze, or you can wait until the Hydrocal sets and break away portions

Fig. 4-2. Water-sprayed sheets of newspapers or paper towels can be used to cover the wadded-up newspapers to define the shapes of the hills.

of the scenery to patch in your corrections. Thus you don't have to gamble on how the final shapes of the scenery will look on the layout. If you are using open-grid benchwork, you may have to temporarily nail some scraps of corrugated cardboard boxes beneath the layout to keep the wadded-up newspapers from falling to the floor. You may also have to nail some similar supports or some scraps of wood trim, lath, or 1 x 1 wood strips to the edges of the table to keep the piles of wadded-up paper towels in place. If the towels are too springy, spray them with water. You may be able to better visualize the shape of the scenery if you cover it with a single layer of paper towels wetted with water. The printing and shadows of the newspapers can be confusing. The layer of plain paper towels, either brown industrial-grade or white household towels, will provide a better image of the actual shapes.

Profile Boards

When the mountains and valleys reach the back and front edges of the table, you are faced with the problem of supporting them. Do not attempt to bring all the scenery to the level of the tabletop. Some areas should rise far above the table edge, while others will require that you cut into the table edge to provide space for deeper valleys. If you use open-grid benchwork (see Figure 3-3), you won't actually have to cut into the benchwork unless you decide to create some very deep canyons. The newspaper mock-ups show you precisely where the mountains and valleys will be at the front and rear of the table. In effect, the table edges slice right through the scenery to produce a profile of the mountain or valley at that particular point. Many modelers make a rough-edged cut in a board to finish the edge of the table. The boards are called "profile boards" because they trace the profile of the scenery at that point (Figure 4-3).

Profile boards can be cut from 1/8-inch-thick plywood or from a hardboard like Masonite. Seal the boards thoroughly with latex paint before applying the plaster scenery. If you prefer a rock-like effect along the edges of the table, nail or screw the profile boards to the *inside* edges of the table. The Hydrocal plaster can be draped over the profile boards and pulled right down to the table edges. The resulting vertical cliff can then be detailed to represent rocks. You can decide whether the cliff faces are supposed to represent the strata revealed when someone cut the access aisle through the scenery or just a rock cliff complete with some weeds and perhaps a small rivulet or waterfall.

Mixing Plaster for Thin-Shell Scenery

If you enjoyed playing with mud pies as a child, you will probably enjoy working with plaster. You cannot work with plaster without getting it up to your wrists, if not your elbows. To help keep it off your skin, purchase some elbow-length rubber gloves or one of those rub-on coatings that mechanics use. And always wear old clothes. The conventional system of American measures is listed on Reference Card 5 to help you keep track of how much of everything you need. Measure what you use and make a note of it so that you can repeat your results. Use a Pyrex mixing pan for plaster because it is easier to clean after the plaster sets than conventional glass. As an alternate, use flexible plastic pans, but keep in mind that some of the dust from the set plaster will remain in the pores of the plastic.

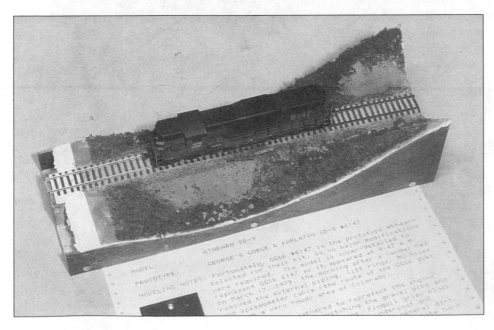

Fig. 4-3. George Booth used Masonite profile boards on his simple 4 x 18-inch diorama. This gave him the freedom to model both a cut (right) and a fill.

Always, always add plaster to water. This method prevents the plaster from forming into hardened piles in the pan. Of course, you must continue to stir as you add the plaster to the water. Also you should color the water, rather than adding powdered color to the plaster. Precoloring the plaster is extremely important: if you use white plaster, it will be nearly impossible to color every nook and cranny, and patches of white will be visible from various viewing angles. Even the master model railroader and scenery caricature expert John Allen made that mistake on his first two railroads. The snowy white patches of plaster looked like snow, a disturbing effect on the summer scenes.

Plaster-Setting Retardants

Don't be afraid to experiment with retardants to delay the setting time of the Hydrocal or, when you install rock castings, to delay the setting time of the plaster of paris or molding plaster. You know that you need a retardant when you find that the plaster in your mixing tray begins to harden before you are finished. Actually, you have two choices: Mix less plaster or Hydrocal, or mix the same amount and add some retardant. There are two extremes here: You may mix as little as a two-ounce paper cupful of molding plaster if, like Dick Shurberg, you want to hand-carve rockwork, or you may want to mix as much as a half-gallon of Hydrocal if you want to cover a large mountainside in just one evening.

If you must retard the setting time of Hydrocal, you have only one alternative: Buy the U.S. Gypsum (the makers of Hydrocal) retarder that is designed especially for use with Hydrocal. Any other kind might weaken the set Hydrocal. For conventional plasters, such as molding plaster or plaster of paris (almost identical plasters), use either white household vinegar or hydrous citric acid from a large drugstore or chemical dealer. The amount of retarder is something you must experiment with; it can range from as little as 1/2 ounce per 128 ounces to as much as 1/2 ounce per 8 ounces, depending on your climatic conditions and just how long you must delay the setting time. In general, the more retarder you use, the weaker the plaster will be after it sets.

Making Mountains

It's now time to get up to your elbows in plaster. If you are working with Hydrocal-soaked gauze, color the water, then simply submerge the Hydrocal-soaked gauze in the colored water for one minute, then apply it to the scenery. Start with a quart of water and however much coloring and Hydrocal is necessary to make a mixture about the consistency of whipping cream. Tear the paper towels into strips about 4 x 12 inches until you have enough to cover at least two square yards. Do this *before* mixing the

plaster. Dip the torn paper towels into the colored Hydrocal mix and drape them over your newspaper scenery (Figure 4-4). Overlap at least half of each towel (Figure 4-5). Repeat the dipping and overlapping process until you run out of the first mix of Hydrocal.

Keep a gallon bucket of water on hand so that you can immediately rinse out the pan and the mixing spatula before making a second batch. Mix this batch exactly like the first, and cover the area you just finished with a second overlapping layer of Hydrocal-soaked towels. You will then have at least three (usually four) layers of Hydrocal and paper towels in every area of the scenery. Just two layers of the Hydrocal-soaked gauze are needed. This is the minimum for self-supporting scenery. If you are covering only a square foot or so of open space, you may be able to get by with just the first two overlapping layers. Cover every inch of scenery, even those areas that will become rock cliffs. Remember, though, to keep the Hydrocal layer far enough away from the tracks or proposed structures to leave space for rocks.

It should be obvious by now that working with plaster is a messy business. You must protect the track and any structures against splashing plaster. The track itself can be covered with a 3/4-inch strip of masking tape for N or HO scale track. This is one reason why many modelers ballast their track only after the scenery and coloring and textures are complete. It's easier not to have to worry about other scenery up to the edges of the ties than to try to protect the ballasted edges all the way through the scenery process. If some bridges must be left in place, they can be covered

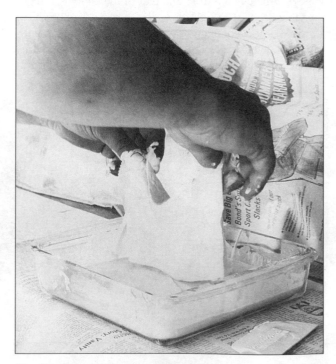

Fig. 4-4. Dip and thouroughly soak the paper towels in the creamy Hydrocal.

Fig. 4-5. Overlap the towels by about half to prevent any thin areas or holes.

with plastic wrap or Baggies. Saran Wrap is best for protecting tunnel portals because it can be tucked in close to areas that will receive plasterwork (Figure 4-6).

Use pieces of flat plywood or hardboard cut to the size of any building sites. Include enough space for adjacent roads or parking lots. These pieces can be supported by wadded-up newspapers or nailed to the track as subroadbed. Roads can be constructed from corrugated cardboard to give them a flat surface, and that surface can be coated either with plaster or Hydrocal until the final layer of plaster or papier mâché is applied. Unless the foundation of a building is on sloping land, such as a mine, remove the building during the Hydrocal application process. The

Fig. 4-6. Protect tunnel portals with plastic wrap (like Saran Wrap) before covering them with the Hydrocal-soaked towels.

base of the building can be buried later during the application of dirt or other scenic textures. If you must cover the base of a mine, trestle, or other structure with Hydrocal, cover the rest of the structure or bridge with Saran Wrap. Of course, the entire work area should be covered with six or more layers of newspapers to make cleaning up easier. You may also want to mask the edges of the benchwork with masking tape and paper towels. If you know in advance that the cleanup will be easy, you'll find that working with Hydrocal or plaster is actually fun.

Rocks and Cliffs

Nothing looks more like a real rock than a real rock. However, a real rock seldom looks like a scale-model rock. The texture of the rock may be perfect, but its color is made up of sand-size particles that are the size of boulders in a 1/87 scale environment. What you need is the best of both worlds—the texture of real rock and the proper colors for a miniature scene. You also must be certain that you are using these rocks in their proper places so that they do form cliffs or outcroppings.

Model railroaders have developed a five-step technique for duplicating the texture of real rocks and their color. (1) A latex rubber mold is made of a portion of a real rock (or a real piece of coal or driftwood); (2) a mixture of powdered plaster, color, and water is poured into the mold; (3) the plaster is slapped against the scenery so that the rock can bond to the scenery and bend slightly to conform to its shape; (4) the rubber mold is peeled away the moment the plaster just begins to harden; and (5) the rock is stained with a dark brown, reddish brown, or gray stain to accent the cracks and crevices. That's all there is to it. Color-Rite, Superior Hobby Products, Woodland Scenics, and other firms even make the rock molds for those who want to skip this step. For rocks in small dioramas or those that would go to the edge of the layout, you can use the weathering technique in Chapter 11 to produce more color variations. You will also want to texture the lower edges of any cliff with small pebbles or talus made from broken-up leftover plaster colored to match the rock cliffs.

Rubber Molds for Rock Castings

The process of making a latex rubber mold to create plaster castings goes back nearly to the 1940s. Latex is a special liquid that vulcanizes, or cures, at room temperature, and it is sometimes referred to as RTV (Room Temperature Vulcanizing). There are several industrial compounds available, but those suitable for modelers are sold by craft supply stores (for casting plaster or clay figures in homemade molds) and by many model railroad shops under the Mountains-in-Minutes, Activa Insta-Mold, Superior Hobby Products, or Woodland Scenics labels. Follow the instructions on the label of the liquid latex or RTV liquid.

You will need a small roll of cotton gauze to reinforce the mold and a spray can of silicone lubricant to serve as a mold-release agent. Select a suitably textured rock, piece of broken coal, or driftwood (see Chapter 2). Your molds should range in size from a minimum of about 4 x 4 inches to a maximum of about 9 x 12 inches, so you won't need a very large rock or piece of coal as your master pattern. Also, you can overlap and rotate the plaster castings to produce as large or as small a rock cliff as you need. Remember that there is no substitute for a photograph of the real rock cliff to give you a general idea of the texture and relative positions of the fissures and cracks in the real rock face. Most modelers are satisfied with no more than a half-dozen different rock molds taken from several different textures of real rocks.

To make the latex or RTV mold, spray the area you want to duplicate on the real rock with several thick coats of silicone lubricant. Let it dry for at least an hour. Use a disposable paint brush or wooden tongue depressor to smooth a layer of the latex or RTV about 1/16 inch thick over the portion of the real rock. Let this first layer cure completely, then apply a second, thinner layer and cover it with two pieces of gauze. The gauze should sink into part of the still-wet latex or RTV. Next, cover the gauze with another 1/16 inch or so of latex or RTV, and let those last two applications cure completely. Repeat the latex/gauze/latex process at least once more for molds smaller than 6 x 6 inches, and add a third layer for molds larger than about 6 x 6 inches. The gauze, embedded in the several layers, reinforces the mold so that it won't rip when you remove it from the later applications of plaster.

When the latex has cured completely, gently peel the mold away from the rock. Small chunks of the latex or RTV will be caught and torn away where they were em-

bedded in the cracks and fissures. Don't worry about them because they won't noticeably affect your model rock textures. Let the mold dry for three or four days before using it again. Store all your rock molds in a box large enough to hold some of those pesky Styrofoam peanuts or discs used for packing. The molds will weaken and tear if they are folded.

Although Hydrocal can be used for rock casting, it is too hard and dense to approximate a realistic texture when stains and paints are applied. For lightweight scenery, however, it may be worth the trouble to make the thin-shell rock castings from either Hydrocal or Woodland Scenics Lightweight Hydrocal as described in Chapter 5. Molding plaster is available at lumber retailers. If the bags are too large for your needs, substitute the nearly identical (but more costly) plaster of paris sold in hardware stores. You will want the castings to cure relatively rapidly, so you probably won't need to use any retarder for rock casting. You might want to use retarder if you intend to carve your own rocks or if you intend to carve the castings to blend them into an adjacent hand-carved area. Be sure to mix some powdered color or dye into the water (see Reference Card 6) so that the *dry* plaster looks like colored chalk. You will want to add some stains and highlights to the rock, so don't make the plaster as dark as you would for earth surfaces.

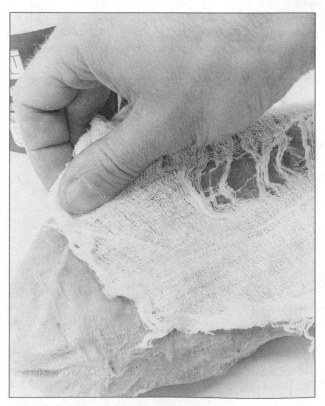

Fig. 4-7. Coat the mold with a few layers of latex paint before pressing on the first layer of gauze.

Casting Directly on the Mountain

Fill the mold only with about 1/4 inch of plaster. Try to judge the amount by pouring the water into the mold first to see how much is needed, then pour it into the mixing pan. This mixture can be just a bit thicker than that used for thin-shell scenery. The plaster should be just thin enough so that you can pour it from the mixing pan without any lumps. If you make it too thick, it won't reach the tiny detail areas of the mold. If you make it too thin, you will have to wait too long for it to cure, and you will spill the plaster on your way from the pouring area to the Cliff.

Instant-Setting Plaster/Water Mixture

It may take as long as 15 minutes for the plaster-filled rock mold to harden from the mud-like state to the firm state which enables you to peel the mold away, leaving the plaster rock firmly attached to the Hydrocal mountain. You can reduce that time by about one-third if you prepare a special water mixture, as the Slim Gauge Guild discovered, *before* mixing the powdered plaster for rocks to be cast in latex molds.

Add about 2 tablespoons of raw powdered plaster to a quart of water; thoroughly color the water so that it looks like milk. Let the water and plaster mix sit, after a thorough stirring, for 20 minutes to allow the plaster to cure. This plaster-treated water apparently provides a catalytic action when the bulk of the powdered plaster is mixed in, reducing the curing time to about one-third that of the usual mixes. (This is the reason it's wise to clean any plaster or Hydrocal mixing containers thoroughly after each batch; the leftover plaster acts much like the treated water I've just described to accelerate the curing process.) With some practice, you'll find that the treated water will allow you to slap a plaster rock of muddy consistency onto the mountains, then hold the latex mold around that rock only about 3 minutes before the plaster is hard enough to retain its shape when you pull the latex mold away. Do remember, too, to pre-wet the Hydrocal mountain with plain water (or detergent water) so the mountain does not leach all the water from the plaster rock before the plaster has time to cure. When applying several (or several dozen) plaster rocks to a single area, the adjacent rocks should also be sprayed with water just before the fresh plaster-filled mold is applied, so the new rock texture will adhere.

The process goes very rapidly, once you understand the timing that's involved. The procedure is to fill the latex or RTV mold with about 1/4 to 1/2 inch of very soupy plaster. Hold the mold and shake and wiggle it to help release any trapped air bubbles while you wait for the plaster barely to begin to cure. At that exact moment, you literally slap the mold and plaster up against the cliff (see Figure 4-8). The plaster will adhere to the cliffside better

if you first spray the area thoroughly with water and about 4 drops of dishwashing detergent per pint of water. Push the mold firmly against the cliff so that the plaster will conform to the shape of your Hydrocal cliff. Don't worry about distorting the shapes of the rocks inside the mold. You want the mold only for texture. The cliff behind the plaster provides the shape.

Hold the mold right there until you can just feel the plaster harden. (It will also begin to give off some heat, but you may not be able to feel it.) It takes some practice, because the sooner you can remove the mold, the easier it will be to get it off without tearing or breaking off the smallest details. If you remove it too soon, the plaster will run and the detail will be ruined. if you do pull the mold off too soon, *immediately* scrape as much of the plaster away as you can, spray the area with more water, and try again. The adjacent areas of rock should overlap the first by about 1/4 to 1 inch, so you may want to keep the plaster in the second mold just a bit thinner (about 1/4 inch) along the edge that will overlap the first rock casting. Pay attention to any grain in the fissures in the mold, and apply the grain at random or keep it parallel to the other castings, depending on the type of real rock you are trying to duplicate.

Throwaway Foil Molds for Rock Castings

The folded and cracked effects of granite and similar types of rocks can be duplicated by using aluminum-foil molds. Cut or tear a piece of foil about 4 x 6 inches. (It's not practical to use pieces larger than about 5 x 10 inches.) Crumple the foil into a tight ball and gently unfold it, then crumple and bend it loosely (see Figure 4-9). The process of making this kind of mold is exactly the same as that for latex or RTV rubber molds. When the foil mold is peeled away, it will probably tear, so a fresh piece of foil must be used. There are two tricks to the foil-mold process: getting those tight little crumples right, and using the same crumpling technique with each foil mold so that the texture does not vary. Nearly all of the scenery on Lee Nicholas's HO scale Rio Grande layout (see Figure 2-1) was made with crumpled-foil molds.

Quick Coloring Tips

Reference Card 8 describes just about every color you will need for rocks, earth, and soil. This chart, and most of the others, is designed for use with various water-base paints. The Polly Scale color charts are sold for about $2 through hobby dealers, or you can order them directly from Floquil-Polly Scale. Alternatively, Sherwin Williams color-chip charts are available nationally, or match them with another brand of high-quality latex interior wall paint. The most important element in scenery is color, and these charts are the key to locating the correct colors. All of the colors on these charts have actually been

Fig. 4-8. Members of the Slim Gauge Guild slap one of thousands of still-wet plaster rock molds and plaster against a mountainside.

matched to rocks, dirt, concrete, blacktop, and sand. *Warning:* Take the color chip charts from Polly Scale or Sherwin Williams outside and match the colors for yourself. You may need to add some white or off-white to any of these color samples to obtain the correct pastel shades for your lighting conditions.

Use these color chips when mixing powdered colors or fabric dyes with plaster or Hydrocal so that your plaster will be similar to the final scenery colors. The dried plaster will, of course, be lighter than when it was wet. Mix the colors so that the dried plaster actually will be a few

shades lighter than your paint-on earth colors. You can also use these earth colors as glue for attaching dirt as well as earth and foliage-colored ground foam textures to nearly all the scenery that is not textured with rock castings (see Chapter 6).

Adding Depth to Rocks

If you added enough color to the water when you mixed the plaster for rock casting, you now have the basic rock color. The color also disguises any chips (or deliberate holes for trees) that might occur later. For most rock

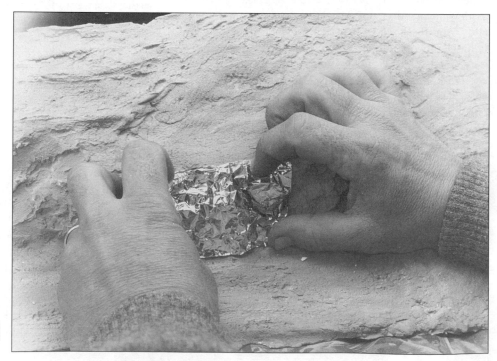

Fig. 4-9. Crumpled aluminum foil can also be used as a mold for casting rocks in plaster.

Fig. 4-10. If you precolor the plaster for the rock casting, you can apply a darker wash to highlight the cracks and texture.

faces, the only additional coloring needed will be a simple shading to bring out the texture of the castings and to emphasize any fissures. Apply a wash of about 19 parts water to 1 part paint, and the color will automatically be deposited in the textures and crevices and washed away from the highlights as the water evaporates. Never use black for the wash color; it will create a harsh, unrealistic salt-and-pepper effect. Select a shadow color from the same family as your basic rock color, only several shades darker. Use brown (rich brown or dark brown, from Reference Card 8) to provide the shadows on beige (brown) rocks. Use reddish brown for rocks that are to be beige (reddish brown), and so forth.

For larger cliffs, you can literally flood the plaster by applying the wash with a basting syringe, available in grocery and hardware stores. Smaller rock outcroppings can be shaded by brushing on a darker wash (Figure 4-10). For close-up detailing, you may want to apply several colors using the weathering techniques in Chapter 11. The Polly Scale paint mixes for spray-painting with an airbrush (Reference Card 7) will provide professional scenery effects.

Retaining Walls and Cliffs

Most model railroaders include far too many rock cliffs in their scenery. Even the brave builders of the narrow-gauge railroads through Colorado's Rockies were forced to bolster the mountains to keep rocks from falling on or out from under the tracks. Consider facing at least one-third of your vertical slopes (any cut, fill, or cliff steeper than about 45 degrees) with a simulated wood, cut stone, or brick retaining wall. Ready-to-use retaining walls are available with propor-

tions suitable for N, HO, and S scale from firms such as A.I.M., Chooch, ColorRite, Mountains-in-Minutes, Mr. Plaster, Brawa, Faller, Kibri, Noch, Vollmer and Woodland Scenics. If you use these preformed, precolored products, be sure to mask their detailed faces with masking tape to avoid plaster droppings or discoloration from the paints and washes you use for the surrounding scenery.

Quarries, Rubble, and Talus

Perhaps the most difficult scenery feature to capture in miniature is a rock quarry. There is a subtle difference between the way rock is removed from a quarry and the way it is blasted from a rock cut for a railroad right-of-way. The type of stone being quarried can also make an incredible difference in the appearance of the quarry walls. There is almost no similarity among marble, flagstone, and sand quarries. Open-pit mines fall into the same category, Try to visit a quarry or find color photographs of one. Or obtain a sample of the type of stone being quarried to use as your model. In many cases the quarried stone is several shades *lighter* than the surrounding natural cliff faces. The natural faces appear to be wet examples of the dry colors of the quarried stone. In some instances, the colors are the same.

Remember to add plenty of rubble, smaller chips and stones that have dropped to the bottom of any cuttings. The leftover colored plaster from the rock cliff can be placed in a cloth bag and crushed into scale-size (3- to 24-inch-square) chunks of rock. Color the rubble with a wash of the same color used to highlight the cliff faces. When rocks are washed from the cliff faces by nature (usually by glacial movement), it is called *talus*. Part of the realism of the Slim Gauge Guild's scenery stems from its wise use of talus.

Fig. 4-11. Richard Zinn's HO scale diorama depicts the Rio Grande Southern's Ophir, Colo., station and log retaining wall.

Fig. 4-12. Dave Riggles carved these steps in plaster. A similar, polyfoam stone wall with steps is made by Mountains in Minutes.

CHAPTER 5

Lightweight Scenery

There is no need to consider the weight of the scenery if you are only building a small diorama. If you are building a larger scene or a model railroad, however, the weight of the finished scene can be important, indeed. Model railroaders, particularly those who are building their layouts in portable sections for frequent moves or who are simply creating one module for a modular layout club, have developed several techniques for building lightweight scenery. Most of these techniques have become accepted for use in building any scene so they have already been discussed in Chapter 4. If light weight is a primary concern for your large diorama, scene, or layout, you may want to be aware of these more successful alternative methods of scenery construction.

Featherweight Mountains

The easiest way to create lightweight scenery is to stack layers of extruded-polystyrene (Styrofoam is a common brand) to make contours (described later in this chapter). The thin-shell Hydrocal plaster-soaked paper towel technique, however, can also produce scenery almost as light as any scenery made using Styrofoam sheets. Substitute Woodland Scenics Lightweight Hydrocal plaster for conventional Hydrocal to create a somewhat lighter-weight version of the thin-shell technique. If you prefer a simpler method of creating thin-shell lightweight scenery shapes, use the plaster-impregnated gauze like Activa's Rigid Wrap or Woodland Scenics' Plaster Cloth in place of any type of Hydrocal and paper towels.

Choosing the Best Lightweight Scenery

The Hydrocal-soaked gauze saves enough weight, as compared to conventional Hydrocal, to make the two layers of Hydrocal-soaked gauze one of the lowest-weight methods of shaping scenic contours, including hills, valleys, and mountains. The plaster-soaked gauze is so strong that two layers of the material are enough to about match the strength of three or four layers of Hydrocal and paper towels. The plaster-soaked gauze is a bit more expensive than other materials for shaping scenery.

It is virtually impossible to determine which of these three methods (extruded-polystyrene contour boards, Hydrocal-soaked paper towels, or Hydrocal-soaked gauze) produces the lightest scenery because no two areas of scenery have the same shapes and sizes. None of the three techniques, however, need any massive support from beneath the layout, and none requires the use of screen to shape the hills and valleys.

The expanded-polystyrene or extruded-polystyrene foam insulation board method of starting with contours allows you to construct the scenery as though you were recreating a topographic map, one contour at a time. It is more difficult for most people to envision what the scenery will look like with this method. If you use the Hydrocal-impregnated gauze, however, the hills and valleys can

Fig. 5-1. Four 1-inch layers of extruded-polystyrene form the basic contours for a tunnel. Cast "Thin-Shell" Lightweight Hydrocal plaster rocks will form the portal around the tunnel mouth.

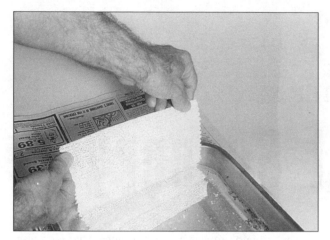

Fig. 5-2. The plaster-impregnated gauze is dipped in water then draped over the wadded paper mountain shapes almost exactly like the "Thin-Shell" Hydrocal in Chapter 4.

be shaped with wadded-up newspaper covered with wet paper towels. Effectively, you mockup the scenery in full size, changing and adjusting mountains and valleys by pushing paper here and adding a pile of wadded-up paper there, until the shapes are exactly what you desire. All the techniques are shown in Chapter 4. Woodland Scenics has a lightweight scenery and layout-construction system called "SubTerrain" (Figure 5-3) that uses white expanded-polystyrene boards as contour and track supports for Hyrocal-soaked gauze scenery.

The amount of mess produced by all three methods is also about the same. The foam boards must be shaped with a saw or a hot-wire cutter, and the resulting pulverized foam is static-charged, so it clings to clothes. Fur-

Fig. 5-3. The Woodland Scenics' SubTerrain system utilizes comb-shaped Risers and Inclines to support the railroad track and roadbed or roads, with expanded-polystyrene foam boards to shape the scenery contours and the grooved Profile Boards on the edges of the layout. The scenery is shaped with Hydrocal-soaked gauze like Woodland Scenics' Plaster Cloth.

ther, the surface of the shaped-foam boards must be coated with a thin layer of plaster, some other molding compound or the felt Grass-That-Grows material (Chapter 6) for texture purposes. I would suggest you try each of the three methods on some small dioramas to determine what one works the best for you, and simply let ease-of-use guide your choice.

Featherweight Boulders and Rock Cliffs

The large rock faces, cuts through hills or mountains, and cliffs can be some of the heaviest portions of the scenery. I have already cautioned you not to use real rocks because they are simply too heavy and unwieldy, even for a small diorama. if you use plaster for rock castings, however, they can easily add so much weight that it will quickly offset any weight you might save by creating lightweight hills and valleys. You have two choices: buy the lightweight ready-to-use expanded foam rocks from Mountains-in-Minutes, or use the latex rubber molds described in Chapter 4 to make thin-shell rock from Hydrocal.

Cliffs, Cuts, and Other Exposed Rock Faces

If you opt for the Mountains-in-Minutes pre-formed rocks, the rocks should be worked into the scenery before the paper towels and Lightweight Hydrocal are draped over the contours of the hills and valleys. That means that the rocks must be cut, fitted, and held in

Fig. 5-4. The Mountains-in-Minutes cast-urethane rocks can be cut quickly and easily with a hacksaw blade.

Fig. 5-5. Jim Ely used Mountains-in-Minutes pre-formed polyfoam rock moldings for all the exposed cliffs on this HO scale module.

place with temporary supports or tape. If you are going to use the foam board contour method of creating hills, shown later in this chapter, the hills can be cut out to accept the rock castings just before the final layer of texturing is applied. With either method of scenery shaping, however, the Mountains-in-Minutes rocks must be covered with clear plastic or Baggies while the messy surface texturing is being applied.

If you are going to add rock faces using Hydrocal poured into latex rubber molds, the rock faces can be added after the scenery is shaped and is ready for texturing. This method requires the same techniques for adding rocks to either contour-shaped scenery shapes from sheets of foam or for scenery shapes formed from Hydrocal-soaked gauze.

Thin-Shell Rock Castings

You can make your own lightweight rock castings using Hydrocal. The techniques for making your own rock molds and for using the molds to make cast plaster rocks are shown in Chapter 4. If you want lightweight rocks, however, the rubber mold should be filled with just a thin layer of Hydrocal. You can use conventional plaster for thick rocks, but for thinner rocks, plaster is just not tough enough. You will probably have fewer crumbled rock castings if you use Hydrocal.

To create a lightweight thin-shell rock, mix a small batch of Hydrocal plaster to the consistency of thick cream. Fill the latex or RTV rubber rock mold with the fluid, and gently sway the mold from side to side so

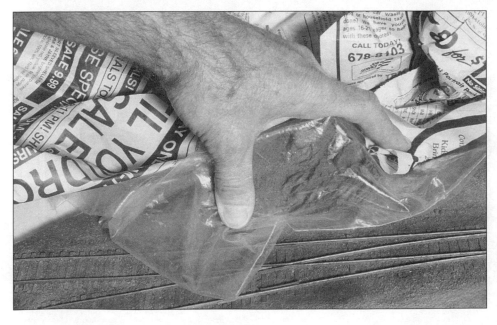

Fig. 5-6. Protect any of the Mountains-in-Minutes cast urethane foam rocks with clear plastic before covering the area with either paper towels dipped in Hydrocal or plaster-impregnated gauze.

Fig. 5-7. Pour a thin layer of Lightweight Hydrocal into the RTV rubber mold and turn the mold to coat the entire inner area with the plaster.

some of the fluid sloshes out the sides. Maintain the movement as the Hydrocal plaster begins to harden. Your goal is to leave about 1/4 inch of adhered plaster on the sides of the rubber rock mold so the center remains hollow. If you work very quickly, you will be able slap this rock up against a cliff during the few instants when the plaster is dry enough to be tacky but wet enough to be flexible. If that technique doesn't work for you, simply let the plaster harden, peel back the mold, and cement the finished rock into the scenery with some more plaster. Obviously, the slap-it-on technique will get the rocks onto the scenery with less additional plaster, and the rocks will likely be easier to shape into a credible cliff, especially if you have an 8 x 12-inch or larger area to cover with plaster rock castings. When the plaster rocks have hardened, stain them with acrylics and water washes as described in Chapter 4.

Contour Modeling for Lightweight Hills

The contour method of modeling hills and valleys is the one used on the U.S. Geological Survey's topographic maps. When the above-sea-level elevation lines are converted into three dimensions, a stair-stepped model similar to that in Figures 5-1 and 5-8 is the result. For some architectural and topographic land models, this type of contour modeling is enough. For most models, the vertical slopes between contours should be blended into more realistic hillsides and cliffs. Thanks to the easy-cutting nature of the polystyrene foam insulation board, it's relatively simple to shape slopes with a serrated paring knife,

Fig. 5-8. The shape of these hills follows the same contours and elevations of U.S. Geological Survey topographic maps.

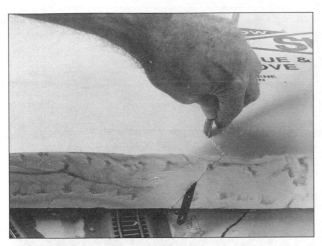

Fig. 5-9. Use a hacksaw blade to cut the blue extruded-polystyrene or the white expanded-polystyrene.

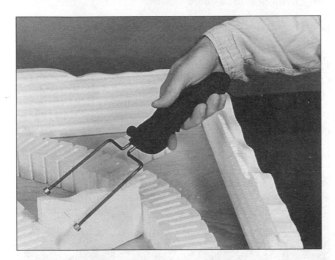

Fig. 5-10. Woodland Scenics' Foam Cutter has a heated wire that will cut polystyrene foam boards quickly with little mess.

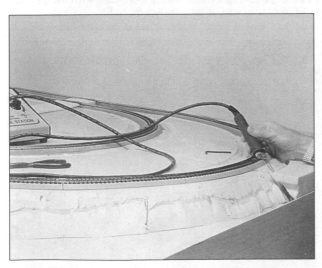

Fig. 5-11. The Avalon Concepts hot-wire cutter has a Detail Station with a variable-temperature control and a DetailWand on a cable that can be used like a knife to cut any polystyrene foam boards.

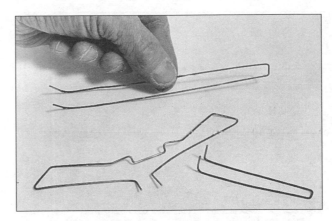

Fig. 5-12. Use needlenose pliers to bend your own "blades" for the Avalon Concepts Detail Wand, using their nichrome wire. The 5-1/4-inch hot-wire blade (top) is used to make shallow-angle cuts for shaping scenery. The sawtooth-shaped blade (lower left) is bent to cut drainage ditches on both sides of HO scale railroad track and roadbed. The shorter U-shaped blade (lower right) is bent to produce a perfect 90-degree cut to use, guided by a steel ruler, to make square cuts through a two-inch sheet of polystyrene foam board.

Fig. 5-13. To cut the drainage ditches on both sides of the railroad track and roadbed, clamp the ditch-cutting wire in the "Detail Wand" and adjust the temperature at the "Detail Station" so the heated wire will make steady cuts through the Styrofoam. The U-shaped loop rides on the rails to position the cutting wire.

Fig. 5-14. Shallow hills, between closely spaced tracks, may only be a bit deeper than a single 2-inch layer of the expanded-polystyrene material. Shape all of the slopes with a hacksaw blade or hot-wire cutter and hold them temporarily in place with 3-inch-long concrete nails until you are satisfied with the shapes.

Fig. 5-15. Bridges can be left until the polystyrene foam is shaped to form the fills and embankments leading up to the bridge abutments. Cut the slopes that will be below the bridge with a hacksaw blade or hot-wire cutter, and slice the track from the foam board with a serrated-blade kitchen knife. The polystyrene foam can then be wiggled loose and pulled from beneath the tracks.

Fig. 5-16. The tracks that will be supported by bridges can remain in place while you complete the texturing of the shaped polystyrene foam surfaces. Install the bridge abutments before beginning the texturing, but the bridges themselves can be added after the majority of the scenery is complete.

Fig. 5-17. When you are satisfied with the shape of any valleys, use as an electric saber saw to cut the 1/8-inch plywood edges of the layout to match the contours you have carved into the scenery. Use a scrap of 2 x 2 or 2 x 4 wood between the saw and the plywood so the blade only cuts 1/4 to 1/2 inch into the plywood.

Fig. 5-18. A mixture of latex wall paint and ground walnut shells provides basic "earth."

Fig. 5-19. The "Grass-That-Grows" system begins by covering nearly all the scenery surfaces with beige felt held in place with latex contact cement.

Fig. 5-20. Holes for trees, telephone poles and signs can be "drilled" through the felt and polystyrene foam scenery by simply punching a hole with an awl or ice pick.

Fig. 5-21. The people from Polyterrain created this entire 4 x 8-foot layout from Dow Corning blue Styrofoam sheets (it weighs just sixty pounds). The legs, however, should be replaced with 2 x 4 lumber and a base made for the layout from at least 1/8-inch thick plywood with 1/8-inch plywood profile boards around the sides and Homosate or Upsom board roadbed beneath the track.

a hacksaw blade or a hot-wire cutter (Figures 5-8 through 5-16). The surface must be sealed and textured. You can use common latex wall paint (thickened with ground walnut shells), patching plaster, or compounds like Polyterrain paste or Woodland Scenics Flex Paste covered with real dirt or ground foam for texture. For a rougher texture, cover the bare contoured foam with Form-A-Mountain scenic covering material. For a grassy surface, use the felt Grass-That-Grows technique in Chapter 6.

Polystyrene and Urethane Foam Sheets

The type of lightweight cellular plastic boards used for home insulation are usually suitable for the lightweight scenery shown here. There are three types of foam boards that are most common: (1) the expanded-polystyrene made from expanded styrene beads (often called bead board), like the soft white foam in inexpensive ice chests; (2) the extruded-polystyrene foam like Dow Corning's blue-colored Styrofoam (and similar materials, colored green, pink, or yellow, from other manufacturers); and (3) the more powdery expanded-urethane foam, similar to the material used by Mountains-in-Minutes for their pre-cast lightweight rocks. The foam is usually sold in 2 x 8- or 2 x 10-foot sheets, in thicknesses of one or two inches. Modelers generally prefer the blue-colored extruded Styrofoam type of foam insulation board. This material is a bit less likely to crack if bent, and when shaped, it does not produce quite as fine a powder as the bead board or the urethane foam. Any of the three types of foam board can produce suitable results, but the urethane foam boards are not recommended for this purpose.

All these materials produce dust when cut, sawed, or sanded, so always work outdoors. The dust can be toxic, so wear gloves and a face mask or respirator. The panels can be cut with a serrated paring knife or a hacksaw blade held with a gloved hand. Many glues will dissolve styrene foam; wallpanel adhesive, usually sold in cartridges for inexpensive caulking guns, works best to cement the foam layers together. Latex-type contact cement also works well. Woodland Scenics' Foam Tack, Liquid Nails For Projects and Foam Board, and Polyterrain's paste are also suitable to cement layers of foam without damage to the foam. Whatever you use, test it on a scrap of foam first. All of the low-odor, water-base texturing and bonding formulas in the Reference Cards will work well with the foam.

Familiarize yourself with the contour technique before cutting the foam panels. Compare the contour lines on the map to the hillside so that you can see why the lines of a steep slope are spaced more closely together than a gentle slope. You can remove material from the inside of hills or mountains when you cut the contours in the foam panels to save weight, to make the material go farther (the cut-outs from the lowest slopes can form the smaller contours for the peaks), and to provide access. Backpacking shops usually supply U.S. Geological Survey topographic maps for the local area.

Cutting Polystyrene Insulation Boards

The blue extruded-polystyrene insulation board or the white expanded-polystyrene insulation board can be cut with a kitchen knife with a serrated blade, a hacksaw blade, or with special hot-wire cutters from Avalon Concepts, Plastruct, or Woodland Scenics. If you are producing mountains on a flat tabletop, cut the polystyrene into contours that match the shape of the hillsides as shown in Figure 5-8. If you are carving a valley or canyon, start with a flat surface and cut into the surface as shown in the color section.

The serrated knife can be used for cutting one-inch or thinner polystyrene insulation board, but it's a lot of work to make deeper cuts. It is much less work to use a hacksaw blade for cutting this material (Figure 5-9). Hold the blade in your fingers or buy one of the handles that are designed to hold just one end of the blade. The knife or hacksaw will, however, produce a nearly weightless powder that will stick to just about anything. Keep a vacuum cleaner with a flexible hose handy to clean up as you cut.

Hot-Wire Cutters for Polystyrene Insulation Boards

The white expanded-polystyrene and blue extruded-polystyrene insulation boards can be cut quickly and with nearly no mess using a heated nichrome wire. Woodland Scenics' Hot-Wire Cutter, Plastruct's Craft Hot-Wire Foam Cutter and Avalon Concepts' Detail-Wand are three hot-wire cutters designed for use by hobbyists. The hot-wire cutter produces a 1/16 to 1/8-inch wide cut, with only a few drips of melted-plastic foam and wisps of white smoke. The hot wire softens the microscopic air bubbles that are trapped in the polyfoam to produce the cut. Use very gentle force to push or pull the heated-wire through the polystyrene foam board so the heat has enough time to work—you are cutting with the heat that radiates from the wire, you are not actually cutting with the wire. If the tool has adjustable temperature, turn the heat up or down so the wire can melt through the polystyrene foam board at about the same speed as you could saw through a piece of 1/4-inch plywood with an electric saber saw. The hot wire produces fumes that can be toxic, especially to anyone with allergies, so always work outdoors. Also, be careful of the drips of molten plastic because they can burn skin and, if they drip on the polystyrene foam board's surface they will melt through the polystyrene. It's wise to wear gloves and long sleeves to protect your skin.

The Woodland Scenics' Hot-Wire Cutter (Figure 5-10) looks like a small jigsaw, but the "blade" is a heated wire and the current to heat the wire is supplied by 110-volt current that powers the transformer built into the tool's handle. The Plastruct Craft Hot-Wire Foam Cutter

is similar, but it is powered by two flashlight batteries, so it's working life is limited to the life of the batteries. These tools are fine for cutting nearly right angles through polystyrene foam boards.

The Detail Avalon Concepts DetailWand (Figures 5-11 and 5-13) is more expensive than the other tools, but it is far more versatile because you can make your own "blades" from the 12-inch lengths of wire supplied with the tool. The DetailWand has a separate 110-volt "Power Station" transformer with adjustable temperature control for the hot wire. The DetailWand connects to the Power Station with a heavy-duty electrical cable so the Detail-Wand can be handled like a knife.

I made three separate "blades" for the DetailWands shown in Figure 5-12: two squared-off U-shaped pieces, one 5-1/2-inches long and one 2-1/2 inches long, and a third zig-zag-shaped piece for cutting drainage ditches or borrow pits. The 2-1/2-inch blade has its attached tabs bent to produce a precise 90-degree or right-angle cut and it is used to make precise square cuts through 2-inch-thick polystyrene foam boards. If the Detail Wand is guided with a steel ruler, the cut will both straight and vertical. The 5-1/4 inch blade has the tabs bent at about a 30-degree angle so it can be used like a conventional knife for making deep cuts in the polystyrene insulation board (Figure 5-11). You can use the 5-1/4 inch blade to shape the edges of the contour panels and save the mess of sanding, shaping or wire-brushing. The legs of the U-shaped pieces must be at least 1/2 inch apart so the wires cannot touch when you drag the blade through the polystyrene. If the wires do touch, they can become red-hot and blow the fuse on the Detail Station. If this happens, you are probably pushing the wire too hard or the temperature is set too high. If you remove too much of the polystyrene material with any cut, save the piece you removed and simply glue it back in place.

For the most realistic scenery, the slopes should be no greater than 30 degrees. With a slope that shallow, you will

Fig. 5-22. Even the roadbed for the track is made from 1-inch thick styrofoam on the Polyterrain layout. The addition of a wood base and Homosote roadbed would probably add about twenty pounds but the layout would be far more practical.

need a blade at least 5 inches long to cut through the 2-inch thick polystyrene in a single pass. For even more gentle slopes, make two passes with the hot wire cutter to cut as deep as you can (perhaps just a vertical inch into the material) with the first cut, then vertically down to the bottom of that first cut to remove a V-shaped piece of polystyrene. Make the second pair of cuts to complete the cut through the final inch or so of polystyrene. If the 5-1/4-inch U-shaped blade is bent that 30 degrees at the handle end, you can make cuts that are so shallow they are nearly parallel to the surface of the polystyrene. Remember, you can do this same cutting with a hacksaw blade if you don't want to invest in a hot-wire cutter.

Cutting Borrow Pits with a Hot-Wire Cutter

The zig-zag blade was bent so the shallow U-shape in the center exactly fits across the metal rails of HO scale track. The V-shapes on the extreme ends are bent at about 30-degree angles to match the slopes of the borrow pits or drainage ditches that are common on the sides of railroad grades and highways (see Chapter 3, Figure 3-2). To use this blade, hold the DetailWand vertically over the track with the shallow-U over the tops of the metal track rails. Drag the blade through the extruded-polystyrene and it will automatically cut two shallow V-shaped drainage ditches or borrow pits on each side of the track guided by the track's rails. The drainage ditches are one of the most essential—and seldom-modeled—characteristics of real railroad right-of-way, as well as essential features of most roads and highways. Note: the hot-wire cutter must be bent so there is about a scale 24-foot-wide shoulder at the "tabletop" (dimension "C" in Figure 3-2). About a scale 5 feet of flat shoulder (bare tabletop) should be visible on each side of the roadbed. You may need to make several test-runs with the hot-wire cutter to achieve the exact cuts you desire. That 24 feet happens to be the width of most two-lane roads so the same blade can also be used to make drainage ditches for roads and highways. The road surface itself should be covered with masking tape to define the centerline and path of the road and to insulate the hot wire from the surface of the extruded-polyfoam so the hot wire cuts only the ditches on each side of the road.

The drainage ditches can also serve as a guide to keeping embankments that rise vertically far enough away form the track or highway. The vertical embankments can begin to rise from the bottom of either drainage ditch. Double-check the clearances of any model railroad equipment, however, to be sure the vertical walls are far enough away from the tracks so the longest locomotives or cars do not sideswipe the vertical wall or embankments. The drainage ditches can also serve as guide for

cutting embankments that fall below the tracks; simply continue the cut and angle from the bottom trough of the drainage ditch (Figure 5-11).

Preparing for Bridges

If you are using the extruded-polystyrene for the tabletop of your model railroad or diorama as well as for scenery, there is no need to plan for the locations of valleys or bridges. Start with a base for the railroad right-of-way and highways that is on top of about three layers of 2-inch thick insulation board and you will have someplace to "dig into" when you want to carve the valleys. This method for scenery construction allows you to make decisions about bridges and tunnels after you see that there would be a need for such features. You can, in fact, "add" valleys and bridges even after the track and roadbed are glued in place. First, determine the length of the bridge you want, then wiggle a serrated knife between the roadbed and the top of the extruded-polystyrene tabletop to free the track for the length of the bridge over the valley. Remember that the embankments beneath the bridge should be no steeper than 30 degrees, and make the cuts through the embankment with the hacksaw blade or hot wire. When the valley is cut through, the expanded-polystyrene can be pulled from beneath the track and roadbed. The track and roadbed will be left hanging in the air above the valley just waiting for the necessary bridge and bridge abutments as shown in Figure 5-15 and in the color section.

The photographs in the color section show the tabletop layout made from blue Dow-Corning Styrofoam insulation board for the model railroad layout in the *HO Model Railroading Handbook,* 3rd Edition. They show how the tabletop looks after the foam has been cut with borrow pits for the roads, drainage ditches for the railroad right-of-way, and valleys and hills added to the top of the table with the blue Styrofoam (Figure 5-14). Note that this layout was deliberately constructed from a stack of three 2-inch thick layers of extruded-polystyrene so that valleys and canyons could be cut below the level of the track and roads. The hills were added to the top of the table using the contour method and held in place with concrete nails and glue, but the valleys were simply cut at a gentle angle as shown in Figure 5-11.

If you are building a diorama or simply adding polystyrene scenery to a tabletop, you must protect the edges of the soft polystyrene foam board from chipping. A simple box can be made from 1/8-inch cherry or birch veneer plywood (stores that specialize in hardwood carry the plywood) to surround all vertical surfaces of the layout or diorama. The layout in the photographs was built with just such a 1/8-inch plywood shield around its vertical edges. When the valleys that lie below track level are cut to the shapes you desire, trim the 1/8-inch plywood to match the contours you have created in the polystyrene foam board. Use a scrap of 2 x 2 or 2 x 4 wood (Figure 5-17) as a temporary spacer to allow the blade of an electric saber saw to penetrate only a 1/2 inch or less into the polystyrene foam while the blade is cutting through the l/8-inch plywood.

Shaping the Foam Hills

With the contour technique, the square corners of the wavy contours must be beveled and blended so there is no visible step from one layer of polystyrene foam board to the next. You can use a hacksaw blade or any of the hot-wire tools for this. It is a bit more difficult to use the C-shaped hot-wire cutters like Woodland Scenics' Hot-Wire Cutter (Figure 5-10), but you can shave off a layer at a time and finish the shaping with hacksaw blade. The Avalon Concepts DetailWand with the U-shaped 5-1/4-inch blade can be used like a hacksaw to get the precise shapes in a single pass.

If you are going to create exposed rock surfaces, cliffs or retaining walls, install them before you texture the surface of the polystyrene foam scenery. The pre-cast urethane foam rocks for Mountains-in-Minutes are about an inch or more thick, so you must remove enough of the scenery surface to make room for the thick rock castings. An alternate method of making lightweight rocks, cliffs or retaining walls is to cast the textures directly onto the shaped polystyrene foam with plaster. You can apply wet-plaster cast from latex molds directly to the surface of the polyfoam just as you would to Hydrocal or plaster scenery shapes as shown in Chapter 4 (Figure 4-8) or use the crumpled aluminum foil technique (Figure 4-9) to mold rock faces directly onto the polystyrene foam surfaces. Remember to check for side-to-side clearances on any rocks that rise above the level of the tracks so the railroad equipment does not sideswipe the rocks.

Lightweight Surface Texturing

The shaped surfaces of the polystyrene foam scenery are too rough and porous to be simply painted over and textured. Seal the surfaces with a layer of paint thickened with walnut shells or spread on one of the thicker scenery pastes like Woodland Scenics' Flex Past, Polyterrain's Paste, or American Art Clay's Sculptamold. You can use plain plaster or Hydrocal to seal the surface but it is heavy and likely to crack.

The photos in the color section also illustrate how the entire surface of the foam can be textured with felt, using the "Grass-That-Grows" system in Chapter 6, so there is no need for plaster of any kind, the mess is minimal and the felt surface texture technique is lighter than any of the plaster surface-texturing methods. The entire layout can be covered with beige felt, leaving only the flat, horizontal surfaces for building sites, roads and the railroad track and roadbed uncovered (Figure 5-19). To install the felt,

coat the shaped scenery with a thick layer of latex-type contact cement and press the felt into the still-wet cement. The felt can be trimmed to size after the cement dries. Tease the felt, spray the upper strands green and sift on dirt, followed by a setting spray of dilute artist's matte medium as shown in Chapter 6 and in the color section. With this system, the holes for trees, telephone poles or signs can be "drilled" by simply punching through the felt and the foam with an awl or ice pick (Figure 5-20).

Strength for Foam Layouts and Dioramas

The extruded-polystyrene (Styrofoam) method of scenery construction can certainly be used effectively with conventional model railroad benchwork as seen in Chapter 4. The foam sheets can also become the main support for dioramas and model railroads. The Styrofoam sheets are strong enough to support any type of model scene made with plaster scenery and cast plaster rocks. Because the foam sheets lack edge strength and are easily crumbled, I would suggest that you make a box for the bottom and the outer edges of any scene or diorama module or layout made from Styrofoam. The edges can be plywood as thin as 1/8 inch if the corners are braced adequately and the legs are positioned to prevent sagging (approximately every 30 inches). There's a step-by-step method for building a table like this in the *HO Model Railroading Handbook, 3rd Edition*, and that model railroad is also shown on the color pages of this book.

The Polyterrain Company has used Dow Corning blue Styrofoam to construct an entire 4 x 8-foot layout for HO scale trains. First, a basic gridwork of 15-inch squares was made with 1-inch thick strips of the blue Styrofoam cut into 6-inch strips. The profile boards along the sides were also cut from 1-inch thick Styrofoam. The sheets of Styrofoam were cemented together with Polyterrain Paste, and the same paste was used to cover the shaped scenery. Polyterrain Sculpting Mud was used to cover the vertical areas. The rocks and stones were carved into the Polyterrain Sculpting Mud with a trowel and knife. The loose terrain was held in place with artist's matte medium and the water was made from artist's gloss gel. The company's efforts proved that it is possible to make a layout from this material but, frankly, it's risky. It is difficult to achieve the firm support necessary for model railroad track with the soft Styrofoam, particularly at the turnouts or switches. I would also suggest, then, that the roadbed for the track be constructed from a more rigid material. For instance, use 1/8-inch or thicker plywood with cork, Homosote, or Upsom board for the ballast-shaped area beneath the ties. Or, use the plastic roadbed and track systems like Bachmann's E-Z Track or Life-Like's Power-Loc track. The sides and bottom of the layout can be covered with that thin box of 1/8-inch thick plywood suggested earlier and conventional 2 x 4 legs can be bolted to the edges of the plywood.

CHAPTER 6

Earth, Weeds, Vines and Grass

One of the secrets of realistic scenery is to make sure that every square inch of the plaster surface is covered or colored and textured. Even if you are going to cover an area with grass or weeds, the underlying plaster should be colored. The ground that is visible beneath any stands of trees should be textured to simulate earth (covered with fallen leaves, of course). The surfaces of dirt roads should be textured with real dirt and even the ballast should be placed beneath the railroad track (Figure 6-1).

The best earth-texturing process uses waterbase paint and water-base glue (the bonding agent referred to on Reference Card 13) to minimize odors and to speed up the process so you can apply earth, grass, and weed textures the same night that you install the papier mache, Hydrocal, or plaster earth shapes. If you want to complete a diorama or a portion of a model in an evening or weekend, you can do so without waiting overnight for the intermediate materials to dry. The advantages of the water-soluble system will become more apparent as you add color and texture to the basic scenery shapes.

Earth Colors and Textures

The chart of earth colors on Reference Card 8 provides virtually all the basic hues you might want for any model scene. Use a high-quality latex house paint for all scenery work. Obtain the Polly Scale color charts and Sherwin Williams Decorator color chips. If you cannot locate Sherwin Williams paints or a brand that matches Sherwin Williams colors, simply purchase the Polly Scale chart and match any brand of latex wall paint to those colors. You may also want to buy Polly Scale paints for weathering. Craft supply stores sell other brands of acrylic paints that can be substituted for Polly Scale. Hobby stores may

also carry Badger Accu-Flex acrylic paint that can be used in place of Polly Scale.

Use the latex paint as an earth color *and* as a binder for the layers of texture materials (see Reference Card 9). The system works best if you apply the texture *immediately* after the paint and, for thicker layers of texture, the bonding agent immediately after that (see Reference Card 13). All three compounds—the underlying latex paint, the texture materials, and the bonding agent—are designed to work with either water or alcohol. Any combination of the formulas in Reference Cards 12, 13, 14 and 15 can be applied in one evening. Larger rocks and taller weeds are, in fact, applied *after* the finer earth textures are in place. The larger, taller textures can be applied the same evening, or they can be installed using the bonding agent anytime thereafter. This system of creating textures allows you to finish any given area in a single evening or to come back later to add more superdetails.

Treating, Bonding, and Coloring Real Dirt

Using fine-grind brown foam is a simpler alternative to real dirt. Woodland Scenics numbers 41, 42, and 50 earth foam in fine grinds will convey the impression of real dirt in every application except simulating a well-used dirt road. Woodland Scenics also offers matching shades of a medium-grind foam (number 60) that can be mixed with the finer grades to produce effects such as forest undergrowth and plowed fields.

The simplest way to simulate dirt is to paint the scenery with a thick coat of an appropriate shade of latex wall paint, sprinkle on the ground foam or real dirt, wet the foam or dirt with soaking agent (Reference Card 12), and

Fig. 6-1. With the exception of rocks, cliffs, and river bottoms, all plaster surfaces should be painted and textured for maximum realism.

apply the bonding agent (Reference Card 13) with an eye dropper or spray bottle. You may want to cover portions of some areas with various shades of green ground foam and even flocking or other weed textures at the same time you apply the ground foam. In general, the dirt and the weeds or grass are applied in that order, but *before* the soaking agent and bonding agent.

You cannot hope to be successful with real dirt until you test it, sift it, and treat it (see Reference Card 10). Sift all the dirt through a tea-strainer then sift it through a brass plumber's screen with a 100-size sieve. (Hardware stores and plumbing supply shops sell the screen.) This dirt can be considered dust, too fine for model use. (You can simulate mud by mixing the dust with plaster, adding color to the water when you mix it so that you can be more certain of how the plaster will dry.) After the 100-size sieve, you will have three grades of dirt (in addition to the "dust"): (1) the dirt that did not pass through the screen-door screen can be used to simulate medium rocks found along stream or riverbeds; (2) the

dirt that passed through the screen-door screen but was caught by the tea strainer can be used for rough forest undergrowth or plowed fields; (3) the dirt that passed through the tea strainer but was caught by the plumber's screen can be used to simulate raw dirt and dirt roads and paths. This real dirt can now be applied using the same techniques as those for applying ground foam or track ballast. Be particularly careful to match the color of paint used beneath the dirt to the dirt itself so that you don't alter the color excessively.

It is possible to select just about any color of real dirt and match it to your rocks by mixing the proper color latex paint with the final bonding agent. Mix 1 part latex paint, 1 part artist's matte medium, and 8 parts water with 4 drops of dishwashing detergent per pint of bonding agent. Experiment with this technique on a scrap of plywood because some types of real dirt absorb more color than others. You may have to add more paint to the bonding agent or use a second application of the colored bonding agent.

Ballast and Rocks

You can actually buy rocks. It may sound like the ultimate waste of money, but these ready-sized products may be the easiest way for you to obtain the precise color, sizes, and textures of rock or ballast you need for your layout or diorama.

Each real railroad has a particular color of ballast and that color may vary from one part of the railroad to another. If you can find color photographs, they can be helpful in determining the color of the ballast. Better yet, visit the area and take a sample or two. You may even be able to obtain enough material so that you can crush your own ballast.

Rock crushing, however, can be a time-consuming process. After the rocks are crushed, presumably with a hammer in a cloth bag, you then need to sort out the sizes. That means you'll need to find a variety of mesh screen sizes so you can sort out, for instance, one-inch-scale rocks for use as gravel, two-inch scale rocks for ballast, and four-inch-scale rocks for talus or scree. You'll want to test the rocks using the techniques on Reference Card 10.

You can choose, instead, to buy what you need. Smith & Sons and the Rock Quarry sell about 20 different colors of rock in about a dozen different sizes. A penny paper bag of rock will go a long way if you are only using it to texture a river bed. Woodland Scenics, Life-Like, AMSI, and Plastruct also sell rocks and gravel that can be used for scenery. You can also use HO scale size ballast as scree for HO scale. Smith & Sons, the Rock Quarry, Campbell, Faller, Highball, John's Lab, Kibri, Life-Like, Noch, Plastruct, Sun Ray and Woodland Scenics also sell ballast.

Simulating Loose Dirt

The trick in a model scene is to capture the loose look of dirt, leaves, or blades of grass but still have all the materials glued down securely so that they cannot accidentally be blown into the tracks, turnouts, and operating mechanisms of the locomotives.

You can make a piece of plywood look like a miniature plot of the earth, but even a simple diorama should have at least a slight variation in the level ground. You can add undulations to the plywood or other flat portion of a scene by spreading on some Celluclay or papier mâché as described in Chapter 1. Most surfaces of a model railroad will by now be covered with a layer of thin-shell scenery shapes in paper towels and Hydrocal as described in Chapter 4 or the lightweight scenery system described in Chapter 5. The point here is that the textures should be used *only* for texture; if you try to apply a thick enough layer to create shapes as well, you may end up with a heap of ground foam.

Try to limit the thickness of any texture to a fine enough covering so that at least *part* of the earth-colored latex paint is visible *when the scene is viewed from directly overhead.* This crew-cut effect will contribute more than any single item to the effectiveness of grass and weeds. If you are trying to duplicate a well-used dirt road or path, however, you may have to cover the latex paint With about 1/32 inch of material.

The Five-Step Texturing Process

The surface that you are about to texture must be sealed with a waterproof coat of latex paint. This is important when you are texturing a surface made of papier mâché molding plaster or plaster of paris because portions of the cured plaster may accept or leach more of the water or solvent than others, producing unwanted texture effects and unpredictable bonding. If you use this method to texture raw plywood, Upsom board, or Homosite (a cardboard-like wallboard favored for model railroad roadbeds), the board will probably warp from all the water.

Step 1

Paint the surface with latex and let it dry for at least two days. Use the paint full strength from the can, and select a color to match the earth you are modeling.

Step 2

Use latex paint to tint or shade the dirt and texture materials, as well as bond them. Brush on the latex in place of the bonding agent for this step. This bonding coat of latex paint should be thinned with an equal amount of water to help increase the drying time and to make the paint go further. Do not thin it more than 1:1. Work with no more than about two square feet of the scenery at a time so that you can apply all the texturing material before the paint dries. For the first and second texturing process, work with only one square foot of surface area. Spread the paint as thick as you can, but don't allow it to run down any slopes. When the entire square foot is covered with latex paint or bonding agent, you have completed Step 2.

Step 3

This step must be completed before the second coat of latex paint begins to dry. Sprinkle the dirt, weed, or grass textures directly onto the still-wet paint. Use a tea strainer (Figure 6-2) or simply shake the material over the edge of an old cup. if you are applying dirt (whether real dirt or ground foam) and weeds or grass, apply all of the dirt first, then follow up with just enough grass or weed texture to cover most of the dirt. The dirt should still be visible when viewed from directly above-the crew cut effect.

Step 4

This step must be done before the paint has time to dry. Apply the bonding agent to the entire area with an eye dropper if the area is small (Figure 6-3); use a basting syringe if the area is large. You will want to flood the area so that the artist's matte medium is clearly visible between the grains of texture. If the artist's matte medium

leaves a white residue after it dries, treat the area with some soaking agent. Grumbacher's matte medium is one brand that seems to leave less white residue, but there are certainly others that are as effective.

Step 5

This step must be completed immediately so that the fluids from Steps 2, 4, and 5 can all mix together. Spray the area with the soaking agent, using the finest mist possible. Trigger-operated spray bottles used for misting plants work best (Figure 6-4). Apply enough of the soaking agent so that the area seems to be more white than tex-

Fig. 6-2. Real dirt, tested as on Reference Card 10, can be applied by shaking it through a tea strainer.

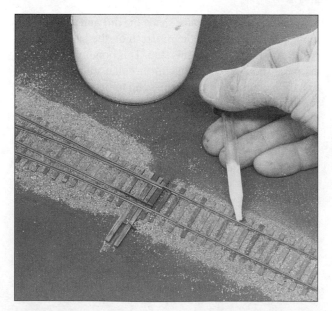

Fig. 6-3. Use an eye dropper (or a basting syringe for larger areas) to apply the bonding agent to the well-soaked ballast or texture.

Fig. 6-4. The techniques used to bond ballast are the same as those used to bond real dirt, ground foam, or any loose material. Spray the loose material with a gentle mist of soaking agent, using a pump-type spray bottle. Hold the spray at least a foot away to prevent material from blowing around.

ture color (Figure 6-5). Allow the area to dry for a day or more, until the white cast disappears, before texturing adjacent areas. Allow the area to dry for at least a week before vacuuming any loose material. Hold a piece of old pantyhose over the vacuum hose attachment to catch any loose texture for reuse. If you want to simulate plowed furrows in a field or ruts in a muddy road, scrape a comb across the field or a finishing nail head down the road *before* the bonding agent dries. The area is now ready for additional weeds, bushes, or flowers.

Weeds, Crops, and Bushes

For purposes of definition, weeds, crops, and bushes are taller than the grasses and low-lying ground covers that can be simulated with the fine or medium grinds of ground foam, but they are smaller than a tree with a visible trunk. There is no single texture better than the various sizes and colors of ground foam to simulate natural plants with leaves. Ground foam reflects light and captures shadows, so it is equally suitable for simulating *clumps* of grass and weeds, pine needles, and most types of leaves.

Using Lichen Moss for Large Weeds and Bushes

The most readily obtainable commercial product for simulating large weeds, bushes, and even the clumps of foliage on deciduous trees is lichen moss. The pretreated moss, sold by firms like Life-Like, Noch, LaBelle, NJ., Heki, Kibri, Model Power, Sun Ray and Woodland Scenics, is usually a special finely tipped moss from Norway. This lichen is noted for its fine leaflike ends. Similar moss is available in the woods of Maine and

Florida, and a coarser moss grows on the north sides of conifers in the Sierras and Rockies. Unfortunately, even the best lichens do not look like leaves. The same is true of sawdust, which always looks like sawdust. Both materials fool the camera, and that's one reason why so much lichen and dyed sawdust is used on model railroads. Use sawdust *only* to duplicate sawdust around a sawmill or timber operation. And whenever you use lichen, cover it with just a trace of fine-grind green foam. There are three stages in making lichen into small weeds, bushes, or foliage on a deciduous tree. Natural lichen must be treated with both a dye (Reference Card 18) and a preservative. Commercial lichen has received both of these treatments, although you may want to alter the bright greens with some yellow or other shades of green. The colors on Reference Card 17 can be used if you spray them on with an airbrush. The glycerin treated, dyed lichen must also be treated with a trace of fine-grind green foam (from AMSI, Faller, N.J., Timber Products, or Woodland Scenics). You have to treat only the visible upper surfaces, so you can merely dip each piece of lichen into a bottle-capful of bonding agent (Reference Card 13). Or you can spray the lichen with cement in an aerosol can, such as 3M Sprayment. (Use this product in a well-ventilated area.)

After coating the lichen with bonding agent or spray cement, dip it in an open box of ground foam (Figure 6-7) and set it aside to dry. After the glue dries, pick up the foam-treated pieces and, one at a time, dip the bottom surfaces into the bonding agent just before placing the lichen bushes into the scene. This foam treatment will allow you to use all of the commercial Norwegian lichen, even the

Fig. 6-5. Apply enough bonding agent so that the entire textured area is flooded with about equal amounts of bonding agent and soaking agent. The bonding agent will dry clear and flat.

Fig. 6-6. Woodland Scenics' ground-foam was used in this farm scene.

coarse pieces. The coarse pieces can be treated with a mixture of medium- and fine-grind foam to produce a variation on the more common lichen-and-foam weeds, bushes, or tree foliage. Use rubberized horsehair or unwoven macrame fiber as a variation on the texture of the lichen (see Reference Card 16).

Sagebrush, Chaparral, and Mesquite

Foam-treated lichen can be used to simulate wild plants by selecting the correct shade of ground foam or spraying the lichen with one of the colors on Reference Card 17. For sagebrush, chaparral, and mesquite, which have only a small branch structure visible, use one of the gray or gray-brown shades of lichen for the plant. Allow the ground foam to represent all the foliage. With this technique, follow the same lichen-treatment steps. The procedure is quick and you can cover several square yards of scale-model hillsides with sagebrush in a single evening. Trim each piece of lichen, rubberized horsehair, or macrame fiber to scale size before applying the ground foam.

Using Real Weeds

Modelers have been searching for decades for natural weeds and other plants to simulate foliage on their model railroads and dioramas. The problem has always been finding a plant in scale size. It's a particularly difficult problem in the common scales used by model railroaders and diorama builders, especially the scales between 1/220 and 1/40 (see Figure 1-4). Actually, there is nothing in nature fine enough to simulate individual leaves, so it's best to use fine-grind foam on the treated tips of lichen. If you are building a diorama in a scale between 1/4 and 1/8, you may find a natural weed or plant that

Fig. 6-7. Put the finely ground foam into an old kit box or bowl, then dip the lichen into the bonding agent and foam.

can be used nearly as is. Only the medium to coarse grinds of ground foam are suitable for these larger scales. Some of the coniferous tree textures in Chapter 7 that are suitable for smaller scales can be used to simulate leaves in 1/4 or larger scales.

When it comes to real weeds, there are a few that can be used for almost any scale. The individual strands or hairs on these weeds are virtually scale size-blades of grass or grass-like weeds. The common weed known as foxtail has individual strands on its seed tips (Figure 6-8) that can be pulled free with tweezers and planted in puddles of bonding agent (Reference Card 13). Some forms of barley grass have a similar tip. The best type is one that used to be sold by the now-defunct firm called Tom Thumb Trees. This is the weed shown in Figure 6-8, although there is little difference between Tom Thumb-style barley grass and any foxtail, except that the typical foxtail is shorter and has fewer hairs. The weed in Figure 6-8 has one important advantage that makes it worth searching for. When you have plucked all those individual hairs and planted them, the core of the plant produces a perfect HO to O scale model of a tall, leafy weed (Figure 6-9). One of the only sources of Tom Thumb barley grass is along the coastal ranges of California. Foxtails, however, grow just about everywhere, and they lack only that textured core; the hairs are still perfectly suitable weeds for scenes like that in Figure 6-8.

Cattails, another common weed, can serve the same purpose as foxtails. The hot dog-shaped brown seed pods that form in the fall contain enough hairlike fibers to cover a scale-size city block (Figure 6-10). Break off one end of the cattail and pick up the clumps of hairs with tweezers to plant them in puddles of bonding agent. The texture and length of the cattail fibers is finer than those from the foxtails, so the two make interesting variations. Both are light beige/brown, but the cattails are a bit lighter. If you want to color these scale-size weeds a shade of green,

do so after planting the fibers with the bonding agent and allowing it to dry for a day or two. Apply the paint with an airbrush, using the colors from Reference Card 17 and the airbrush mixing formula from Reference Card 7.

The field grass synthetic-fiber from Woodland Scenics and Timber Products Wild Weeds can be applied in the same way as cattails. The synthetic fibers are cut to length after the glue dries.

Tumbleweeds, Thickets, and Heath

The tight jumble of medium-size twigs that is typical of tumbleweed and such dense undergrowth as thickets and British heather can be simulated with nearly scale-size materials. One possibility is felt, sold by sewing shops in a variety of colors, including a gray/brown and gray that are similar to the twig colors of many full-size plants. The felt itself can also be used as a grass texture, as shown later in this chapter. Use a metal-bristle brush, such as a file-cleaning card (Figure 6-11) or a steel-wire dog-grooming brush, to brush the individual fibers from the surface of the felt. You'll have to comb and pluck the fibers from the bristles. The clumps of fibers can be loosely formed into balls (tumbleweeds) or collected into large, flat piles to simulate scale-size patches of thickets. The clumps of felt should be sprayed with bonding agent or with a spray adhesive. Sprinkle fine-grind foam over the twigs to simulate leaves.

Vines

The availability of fine-grind foam makes the construction of vines simple: Run a bead of artist's matte medium into wiggly lines and sprinkle on some fine-grind foam. The clump of foliage at the base of the vine can be simulated with small pieces of fine cross-section lichen sprinkled with fine-grind foam. If you want to duplicate

Fig. 6-8. Foxtails, or this type of barley grass, make effective weeds on T. R. Smith's HO scale layout.

Fig. 6-9. Ed Patrone used a barley grass center stalk for the tall weed near the truck door.

Scale-Size Grass

The European brands of flocking made by Kibri, Vintage Reproductions, Noch, and Sommerfeldt are just about the closest thing yet to scale-size grass (for 1/48 through about 1/24 scale) or weeds (for about 1/87 through 1/48 scale). You can cut your own fibers from polypropylene twine (or another macrame product) if you want a slightly longer or shorter fiber. Noch, Faller, and Sommerfeldt offer their flocking as grass mats (Figure 6-12), and nearly every fiber stands straight up like real grass. These mats can be ripped into ragged-edge patches and buried in a mixture of bonding agent, soaking agent, and ground foam, as shown in Figure 6-12. Preiser offers similar plastic-backed flocking that simulates marshes, swamps, and ponds. Kibri, Vintage Reproductions, Timber Products, Noch, and Sommerfeldt also offer loose flocking in plastic bags. Noch even has an electrostatic applicator that allows you to apply the flocking with a spraying action by simply squeezing the plastic applicator bottle (Figure 6-13). You can use the squeeze-bottle applicators to impart an electrostatic charge to the fibers by wrapping a 1/2-inch strip of the flexible, self-adhesive magnets (sold by some hardware stores) around the neck of the bottle. An electrostatic charge makes the individual strands stick straight up when they hit puddles of artist's matte medium. (Use the medium directly from the bottle because it dries with a flat, non-gloss finish.) Only 60 or 70 percent of the fibers will stand straight up, and not as many on the Faller, Noch, or Sommerfeldt flocked paper. For incredible realism, add a few clumps of the foxtail or cattail fibers here and there, then airbrush the area with Polly Scale paints.

freestanding vines that drape from an overhanging rock or from the trellis in a garden, dip a toothpick in water-base contact cement and lift it out to produce strings of glue. You may have to put some contact cement in a paper cup to let it thicken for a few minutes before it will produce the proper length of string. Drape these strings where you want the vines and *immediately,* before the cement can dry further, sprinkle on some find-grind foam in the appropriate shade of green.

Fig. 6-10. The hairs inside a cattail seed pod are perfect for scale-model weeds. Here they are planted on the edge of an epoxy pond just before the epoxy hardens.

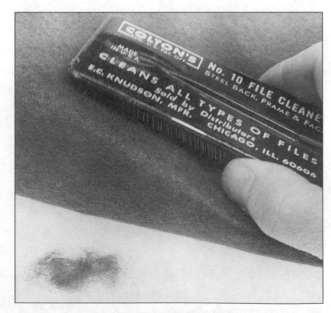

Fig. 6-11. Small tumbleweeds and thick grasses such as heath can be simulated with wool fluff combed from felt with a wire brush.

Felt Fields of Grass

The patches of wild grass that grow on railroad embankments or in abandoned fields are some of the more difficult aspects of the real world to duplicate in miniature. To simulate the random-length weeds in these large fields, use sheets of light beige felt for the system I call Grass-That-Grows. Craft supply stores sell the felt in 8 x 10-inch pieces, or you can buy three-foot-wide lengths of the felt in a sewing supply store. Simply glue the felt over the contours of the scenery with water-based contact cement. Cut V notches where necessary to get the material to conform to the hills and valleys. Try to make the joints in the felt as tight as possible. The gaps can be filled with ground foam or other scenery textures. Let the cement or glue dry for a few days.

Use a wire-bristled file-cleaning brush or a dog-grooming brush to gently tease the strands of felt upward. Use a flicking motion with the brush to get as many of the strands as possible to stand on end. Use scissors to trim any strands longer than about one inch.

Mix some green acrylic paint with about five parts thinner (see Reference Card 17) for application with a spray bottle or air brush as described in Chapter 4 (see

Reference Card 8). Spray the color over the beige felt until you achieve the shade of green weeds you desire. Once again, to get the correct colors and textures, use a color photograph of the real field you are trying to simulate. Don't guess and don't just pick a green at random. Try to color only the layer of beige felt strands you teased, leaving the beige as the dominant color.

Sift some dirt through a flour strainer held directly over the felt. Apply just enough dirt so the felt itself is covered and only the long, teased strands remain visible. Flood the area with a mixture of water and matte medium (see Reference Card 12) to anchor the dirt in place. If you use enough dirt, this system will even allow you to simulate dirt roads or parking lots. In fact, for simulating most gentle slopes, the Grass-That-Grows system may be the only "earth" texturing you need.

Additional textures, including individual strands of flocking or cattail strands, as well as some fine-grind foam, can be sprinkled at random over the area while the matte medium is still wet. These additional textures will simulate different types of weeds and leaves that appear at random in such locations. Allow about a week for the matte medium to dry. Finally, use scissors to trim the teased lengths of the felt to 1/4 inch or so (12- to 18-inch high weeds in HO scale).

Fig. 6-12. Noch-brand flocked paper grass can be buried at the edges in fine-ground foam.

Fig. 6-13. The stand-up effect of the Noch grass paper can be duplicated by applying the flocking with Noch's electrostatic dipenser.

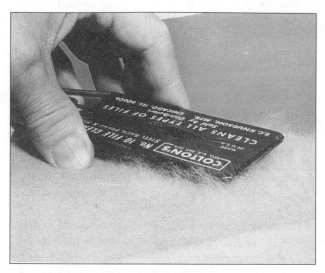

Fig. 6-14. Use a stiff wire brush, like those for cleaning machinists' files to tease the felt so the top layer of fiber strands are fluffed away from the surface of the felt.

Fig. 6-15. Sift real dirt over the teased flet so only the individual grass-like strands are visible.

CHAPTER 7

Trees: From Aspen to Weeping Willow

Realistic trees can be made in only two ways. They can be built by hand from scenery components, or ready-made trees can be modified and repainted. Considering the hundreds of different ready-made trees made by firms like Bachmann, Heki, Faller, Kibri, Woodland Scenics, Noch, NJ., and Life-Like, there would seem to be a limitless variety to choose from. Not so. The best ready-builts have an unnaturally bright green that is too evenly distributed, and there are usually gaps where the branches attach to the trunk. But almost all ready-made trees, including those kits of plastic discs shaped like pine boughs and those faintly disguised bottle brushes, are candidates for realistic trees. There are also several hundred different tree *kits,* and nearly all of them are worthwhile if you take the time to modify them.

Ready-Made Trees

A considerable amount of labor is required to produce even the simplest tree miniature. Ready-made trees are manufactured as inexpensively as possible, and there are basically only two types. One is literally a twisted wire core with plastic bristles, just like a bottle-cleaning brush, covered with ground foam. The length of the bristles and the shape and color of the ground foam determine whether the tree is pine or oak. The second type has a molded plastic trunk and branch structure (much like Woodland Scenics 1100-series tree *kits)* with large clumps of colored lichen moss glued in place. Both types of trees can be converted into realistic models with a good deal of work, but they are not the ideal that you should be striving for when you make your own.

Bottle-Brush Trees

Bottle-brush trees (Figure 7-19) can be effective for simulating a complete coniferous forest that might cover a square yard or two of mountainside on a model railroad. The trees are available in heights ranging from about two inches to nearly a foot, so you can place the larger trees around the edges of your forest and gradually decrease the size of the trees toward the center and toward the tops of mountains to create a forced perspective that will make the forest look even larger than it is (see Chapter 10). There are three steps involved in increasing the realism of bottle-brush trees: (1) bend the wire trunks into slight S bends to simulate the effect of a real trunk; (2) use a pair of heavy scissors to trim the ends of the bristles in a more random pattern, trimming some of the bristles down to their base in the twisted wire trunk; and (3) paint any visible portions of the trunk, including areas where you've trimmed the bristles close to the trunk, and spray the needles with at least two shades of green to give highlights and contrasts (see Reference Cards 17 and 20).

Lichen-Moss Trees

Lichen-moss and plastic-trunked trees can be improved with a similar three-step process: (1) paint the trunks in appropriate shades of brown and gray; (2) dab some full-strength artist's matte medium randomly around the plastic limbs and the lichen, then sprinkle on some medium-grind foam to vary the too-rounded shape of the lichen; and (3) spray the lichen portion of the tree with inexpensive unscented hairspray (work in a well-ventilated area) or dip the tops of the lichen, using the tree trunk as your handle, into bonding agent (see Reference Card 13), then sprinkle on fine-grind foam. The lichen

Fig. 7-1. Ed Patrone used small branches from mesquite, sagebrush, and scrub oak to make the tree trunks for this forest.

trees will always be too thick because of the dense understructure of the lichen that represents the twigs. However, these trees can make nice background details, or they can be used to form the inner portion of a forest where the outer trees were made from kits or scratch-built with a finer, see-through twig and leaf technique.

Simulating Individual Leaves

The Woodland Scenics tree kits include their Foliage Material, which is a fibrous mesh with fine-ground foam already cemented to the mesh so the mesh simulates the twig structure of the tree and the foam simulates individual leaves (Figure 7-2). You can also produce the twig structure with the Woodland Scenics 178 Poly Fiber sprayed with inexpensive unscented hairspray and coated with fine-ground foam to simulate leaves. The fine-ground foam is available in a variety of greens, browns and yellows from AMSI, Noch, Scenic Express and Woodland Scenics. Noch also offers fine-ground flakes that have the flat texture of leaves in a "scatter" material they call "Loose Leaf Flock." The material in the

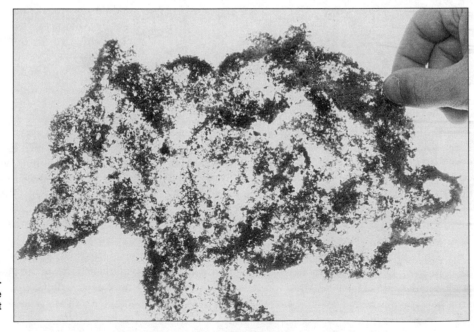

Fig. 7-2. Woodland Scenics Foliage Material should look like this after you have stretched it to its limit.

Noch Loose Leaf Flock appears to be some kind of flakes and ground foam with little or no fibrous material. Do not be misled by the term "flock." Noch and Scenic Express call nearly all their ground-foam materials "flock" Also, K&S Scenery Products offers tiny circular flakes of paper that are about an HO scale 5 inches in diameter dyed in a variety of greens and yellows. The circles are small enough to look like scale model leaves for any scale from about 1/87 through 1/48. Trees made from Noch or Scenic Express tree forms and these Noch and K&S flake "leaves" are shown in the color section. Sprinkle the ground foam or flakes from the top of the tree to simulate the positions of prototype leaves. Keep the foam or flakes away from the trunk. If you do get foam or flakes glued to the trunk, let it dry, scrape what foam or flakes you can away, and brush on more tree-bark gray paint. An alternative—and much more time-consuming method of making individual leaves—is to use the etched-brass leaves shown later in this chapter (Figure 7-22 and 7-23).

Leaf Colors

Determining the correct shade of green for leaves on model trees is an art. There should be no surprise because you are attempting to do just what an artist would do in trying to mix a color in oils or acrylics. In this case, however, we are dealing with not only color, but texture and, the most important element—light. Do not attempt to match the color of an actual real leaf or a blade of grass. The greens will look strange under the artificial light indoors and it is the overall effect and tone you want to capture of a tree full of leaves or a field of grass, not an individual leaf or blade. The colors and textures of the tree or the field of grass alter the colors considerably. The best way to match colors is to use a photograph of the trees your are trying to duplicate that satisfies you. Hold that photograph under the lighting you will use on your layout and match the ground foam to the photograph. The light is reflected by the ground foam and absorbed by the textures to create an overall color or hue. It is that overall effect—not the color of an individual particle of ground foam—that you are trying to duplicate. Obviously, you will need an assortment of the various colors of ground foam to choose from when matching the colors in the photographs. You may, in fact, have to mix two colors to match the shades and tone of the photograph. Remember, it is the overall effect of the color, including both the highlights and the shading, that you want to duplicate. Spread a bit of the ground foam on a index or file card so you can see what it looks like out of the package and in the proper lighting.

Be warned that the exact colors of any of the ground foam can vary from batch to batch. I have found that, under my artificial lighting conditions, the relatively bright green of Noch's 0802 "Loose Leaf Flock" is very close to the right color. Noch makes this same material in a lighter shade of green (0801), a darker green for black oak and other eastern hardwoods (0803), and yellow for aspens and other fall leaves (0804). I also found that a mixture of almost equal parts Scenic Express 805 Grass Green Fine Flock (again, nothing but ground foam—no flocking) and 810 Spring Green Fine Flock was very close to the Noch 0802 color. AMSI's 541 Leaf Green was close but had a bit more blue. To my eyes, under my lighting conditions, this blend is very close to the color of maple, sycamore,

Fig. 7-3. The amount of Foliage Material used on Woodland Scenics Columnar Pine shows how easy it is to alter the texture of a kit-built tree. These trees are similar to the black spruce. *Photo courtesy Woodland Scenics.*

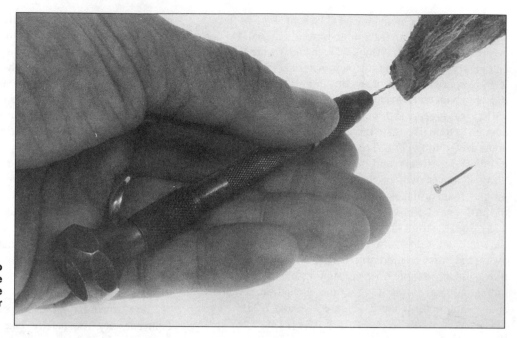

Fig. 7-4. Use a pin vise to hold the drill bit while drilling a hole in the base of the tree trunk for supporting nail.

poplar, ash and beech leaves. The Woodland Scenics 45 Green Grass is the closest color to this in their series of fine-grind foams, but it's a bit lighter than the other green shades. For lighter green leaves like those of aspens, linden and poplar trees, I felt that Noch's 0801 Light Green Flock, AMSI's 441 Grass Green and Scenic Express 801 Light Green were close to the prototype leafs.

Fig. 7-5. Fine steel wire (about 30 gauge) was covered with shreds of steel wool and fine-grind foam by AMSI's professionals to make this 1/24 scale weeping willow tree.

Building Trees from Kits

Model railroad shops carry a dozen different brands of tree kits and nearly 100 varieties of conifers, deciduous trees, and palms. Purchase Walthers' *HO Railroad Catalog,* JMC International's *Source Book* and AMSI's and Scenic Express' catalogs, which contain scenery, tools, and other hobby supplies, to get an idea of the incredible array of tree kits that are available. The tree kits from AMSI, Noch, Scenic Express, Woodland Scenics, Campbell, and Color-Rite include all components, plus instructions, in a single box. You should build at least one of every type of tree kit you can buy at your local shop or through mail order to give you self-confidence and the opportunity to try different techniques. You can then buy bulk quantities of brand-name materials and combine commercial materials with natural or handmade trunks using the patterns in Figures 7-24 to 7-41.

Woodland Scenics' Tree Kits

Woodland Scenics has done more than any other firm to bring easy-to-build, realistic trees into general distribution. The kits contain traditional cast-metal tree trunks. (The less expensive 1100-series kits have plastic trunks, with large clumps of foam to simulate both twigs and leaves.) The cast-metal trunk and large-branch structures are flexible enough to be bent into a variety of shapes, then painted. Woodland Scenics also makes a special foliage material, comprised of brown-gray fibers or hairs (much like macrame fiber) with fine-grind polyurethane foam glued to the fibers. This material makes creating realistic twigs and leaves virtually foolproof. The only trick in using it is to pull it apart and stretch it as thinly as pos-

Fig. 7-6. Inexpensive plastic trees; Scenic Craft's Pine Trees (upper left) and Shade Trees (upper right), a craft store pine (lower left), two pieces of plastic Christmas trees (center bottom), and plastic seaweed (lower right).

sible so that the finished tree has a *see-through* look. An average pad of foliage material, about 4 x 4 inches, should be stretched to about 12 x 12 inches to give the appearance of that shown in Figure 7-2. Work over a newspaper and save the foam that falls off for other scenic textures. You will find that at least 1/2 cup of loose foam remains after you have stretched the material, and that's the way it's supposed to be. With scissors, cut it into small blocks for a deciduous tree or into triangles for a conifer. Dab some undiluted artist's matte medium onto the branches and stick the material in place. Work from the bottom of the trunk upward. Trim any loose strands with scissors.

Work Stands for Simplified Tree Building

Tree kits from Woodland Scenics and some other brands include a pin that protrudes downward from the base of the tree trunk. The pin supports the tree when you plant it in the plaster scenery by drilling a similar-size hole in the plaster. You will need such a pin or nail in any tree. If the kit does not include the pin, or if you are making your own trees, drill a hole in the base of the tree and glue a nail into the hole. The pin is also used to support the tree while you apply the twig and foliage materials. Drill a slightly larger hole in a scrap of wood to hold the pin (Figure 7-4).

AMSI, Noch, and Woodland Scenics Tree Kits

AMSI, Noch, and Woodland Scenics kits have leaves finished with a texture of finely ground polyurethane foam, but the materials for the trunks and twig structure are different. AMSI kits, like most Woodland Scenics

Fig. 7-7. Albert Hetzel assembled this pine tree from a carved balsa wood trunk and air ferns. It resembles the white pine in its shape.

Fig. 7-8. Natural growths are often available at craft supply stores, if you cannot locate them on fall field trips. *Left to right:* yarrow, caspia, air fern (top). Asparagus fern (middle), four pine cones and spirea.

kits, use a cast-metal tree trunk structure, but some of the AMSI trunks are painted and the smaller limbs are easier to bend. AMSI tree trunks are available as separate pieces in a variety of sizes, while Woodland Scenics trunks are sold only as part of a complete kit. Because the Woodland Scenics 1100-Series trunks are plastic, they are not as realistic as the metal AMSI or Woodland Scenics trunks, but they are much cheaper. The plastic trunks must be heated with a flame from a match or cigarette lighter to soften the plastic so that the branches can be bent. This is a tricky process that demands just enough flame to soften the plastic, but not enough to melt it. Too hot a flame can also ignite the plastic itself, so keep a bucket of water handy to drop the tree into, and wear gloves and goggles.

AMSI uses a synthetic fiber, dyed brown, for the intermediate branches. Woodland Scenics No. 178 Poly Fiber is a synthetic fiber similar to macrame used for the twig structure. The fiber must be pulled apart to produce a more open mesh, cut into chunks with scissors, then cemented to the trunk and limb structures with artist's matte medium. Do not use white glue; it leaves a shine, whereas matte medium dries with a flat finish. The fiber mesh can be sprayed with inexpensive unscented hairspray, or dipped into bonding agent (Reference Card 13) and sprinkled with fine-grind foam. The fiber mesh allows considerable versatility in shaping the tree. The illustrations of typical tree shapes in Figures 7-24 to 7-41 show the trunk and limb structure as a darker shape than the twig and leaf

Fig. 7-9. Real mesquite trunks (right). Dead sagebrush (left) also works well for trunks.

portion of each tree. The twig and leaf portion must be shaped with the steel wool or fiber. The ground foam adds only texture, not shape, to kit-built or handmade trees.

Scenic Craft and Other All-Plastic Trees

Molded plastic trees, which are inexpensive and quick to build, are good for areas where several dozen to several hundred trees are needed. The most common tree kits are the conifers from Bachmann (Plasticville), Faller, Pola, Roro, and Kibri. These trees are composed of stacked discs of plastic that simulate tree boughs. Scenic Craft pine trees and shade trees (Figure 7-6) are available in two sizes as one-piece flexible plastic moldings.

Other sources of plastic trees include small pine trees sold by some craft supply stores, pieces of plastic Christmas trees or wreaths, and plastic seaweed sold by pet shops for aquariums (Figure 7-6). These trees can be treated and textured in the same way as the others. All of them have far too many branches, so you must cut one-quarter to as much as three-quarters of the branches from the trunk with scissors. Next, bend the branches at random angles. Scenic Craft shade trees, in fact, can be converted into pine trees by bending all of the remaining branches downward. Spray the trunks and limbs with gray-brown paint, spray the trees with either inexpensive unscented hairspray or dip them in bonding agent, and sprinkle on fine-grind foam. Bach-

Fig. 7-10. Pride of Madera plants (left) make excellent trunk and branch structures for pine trees when covered with small triangles of Woodland Scenics Foliage Material (right).

Fig. 7-11. Caspia weeds can be used as texture and the branch structure if several are grouped into each tree. The shapes of these trees are similar to American elms.

mann, Pola, Roro, Faller, and Kibri pine trees made from stacked discs of boughs should be treated with fine-grind foam in the same manner.

Campbell Tree Kits

Campbell tree kits use a natural growth similar to air fern to simulate the branches and needles on conifers. The kits use a pre-shaped and colored wooden trunk. To assemble, cut the natural growth to length and insert the pieces into pre-drilled holes in the trunks. Drill a hole in the base of the trunks and insert a nail (see Figure 7-4) to support the trees while assembling and planting them. The bright green air fern should be modified by spraying on a wash of gray-green or greenish-yellow (see Reference Card 17). The resulting tree shapes are most similar to white pines (Figure 7-39), but they can be altered to match other species by drilling more holes for more air fern and/or by substituting asparagus fern (Figure 7-8) or foliage material. The flowered portions of caspia weeds can be treated with fine-grind foam and inserted in holes in the trunks to match a real tree with thick, upswept boughs, such as the red pine in Figure 7-38.

Using Natural Growths for Trees

Three general categories of weeds, ferns, twigs, and other natural growths are suitable for miniature trees: (1) growths that simulate only the branch structure, (2) growths that simulate the trunk and major branch structure, and (3) growths that simulate the needles and small limbs of conifers. Figure 7-8 shows the most common growths. The materials used in Figure 7-9 are suitable for a variety of tree trunk and limbs. Figure 7-10 shows the unusual Pride of Madera plant in its dormant state with small triangles of foliage material simulating the boughs of a conifer. Dick Harley and Dave Hussey developed the technique of using the Pride of Madera by trimming its curled ends and gluing on triangles of foliage material with bonding agent.

Ready-Made Trees from Scandinavia

Recently, a weed was discovered in Scandinavia that has nearly perfect trunks and twig structures for scale models' trees in about 1/160 through 1/48 scale. Most of these natural tree forms are between four and eight inches tall, but a few can be as tall as 12 inches. These weeds are packaged as Natural Tree Forms by Noch as a medium-size box (528-23280) or large-size box (528-23800) and are from Walthers and E-R Models. These same weeds are also available by mail order as Super Trees from Scenic Express. The Scenic Express EXP200 Sam-

pler Pack has about as many trees as the Noch medium pack. Scenic Express claims there are 17 to 20 trees in a pack. Scenic Express also offers a 1/4-bushel EXP214 Value Pack that will yield about 35 to 40 trees, or the EXP215 Dealer Case Super Value Pack that will yield about 350 to 400 trees. Scenic Express also has a EXP220

Fig. 7-12. Spray the gray-painted Noch or Scenic Express tree with unscented and inexpensive hairspray, then sprinkle on fine-grind foam or simulated leaf flakes from Noch or K&S Scenery Products.

Fig. 7-13. The trees shown on the cover were made from Noch and Scenic Express tree forms with leaves from fine-ground foam (left), K&S Scenery Products and Noch flake-style leaves (center two trees) and fine-ground foam (right).

Super Tree Starter Kit with an assortment of different ground foam, flakes and colors, artist's matte medium, mixing trays, tweezers and full instructions to make 17 to 20 trees.

The least expensive Scenic Express assortment actually includes complete Scandinavian tumbleweeds (see the color section) just as they are picked in the fields. Pluck the in-

Fig. 7-14. The trunk and branch structure for this tree was made from several pieces of 10-gauge electrical wire covered with water putty and paint. The shape is similar to the oak.

Fig. 7-15. Lonnie Shay carves balsa wood trunks and used caspia (right) for the branches and ground foam for texture. These trees are similar to red pines.

dividual tree forms from the tumbleweed with tweezers (Figure 7-12). The Scenic Express tree forms must be cleaned of a few stray leaves and straightened, while the Noch trees, although about twice as expensive, are already cleaned and straightened. Scenic Express recommends that the trees be soaked in a dilute mixture of water and artist's matte medium to help preserve the tree and to make it easy to straighten. This is a good idea even with the Noch trees, I find that a mixture of about 10 parts water to 1 part artist's matte medium is about right. Submerge the trees in the artist's matte medium and hang them upside down with a clothespin from a clothesline. The weight of the water is enough to straighten most of the trees, but an inexpensive pair of self-clamping tweezers (Scenic Express sells the tweezers, too) can be clipped to the hanging top of the tree to pull it straight while the matte medium dries. The matte medium dries with a very flexible surface which will help strengthen the tree and to preserve it.

When the matte medium has dried completely, spray the trunks and thicker limb structures of the tree with gray paint from an aerosol can or an airbrush. Try to avoid spraying the finer "twig" structure of the tree form so it is not thickened by the layer of paint. Match the shade of gray to the trunk of the tree you are wishing to recreate. Remember that to recreate a specific tree you must match both the color of the bark and the colors of the leaves. These trees' shapes are most similar to aspen, ash, beech or birch trees as-is. If you glue three or four of the slightly bent tree forms together at the "trunk" ends, you can produce the shapes of American Elm, Black Cherry or willow trees. If you glue the Noch or Scenic Express tree forms to a piece of sagebrush (like the etched-brass leaves in Figure 7-20) the trees will produce perfect twig structures for the larger trees like oaks and cottonwoods. For these built-up trees, it's best to use some of the slightly bent Noch or Scenic Express trees to match the shapes of he prototype tree you are modeling.

When the paint is dry, hold the trees by their trunks and spray the twig structure with the least-expensive brand of unscented hairspray, then sprinkle ground foam or flaked leaves over the tree. When the tree is covered, spray it again with the hairspray and sprinkle on a second application of ground foam or leaf flakes. It's that second application of the fine-ground foam that provides the bulk of texture on a foam-covered tree to match the real life trees. Hang the tree by a clothespin while the hairspray dries or stick it into a hole drilled in a piece of wood. When it dries, the tree is ready to plant.

It is seldom wise to use natural growth to simulate the leaves of deciduous trees in any model built to a scale smaller than about 1/40. Natural growth is often fine enough for the trunk and limbs, but the textures usually do not look like scale-model *leaves*. For 1/40 scale or larger, caspia weed can be glued together and a trunk shaped with water putty, a fine plaster-like substance sold by hardware stores. Charles Bowdish and Herman Mike used this technique in Figure 7-11 for the Buhl Science Center's diorama in Pittsburgh. For larger trees, the Buhl Science Center makes trunks and limbs from wire (Figure 7-14) with water-putty bark and makes limbs and leaves from the tips of caspia or yarrow. These same tree-building techniques can be used for trees in smaller scales by shaking or cutting the dried flowers from the ends of the weeds. The fine branch structures can then be grouped into trunks, held with white glue, and textured with water putty. After the trunk is painted, the twig structure of either macrame fiber or foliage material and leaves of fine-grind foam can be added. Lonnie Shay uses hand-carved balsa wood trunks with caspia weed boughs glued into holes that he presses into the soft balsa with a knitting needle (Figure 7-15); the coniferous needles are simulated with medium-grind foams. Caspia and yarrow are usually sold by craft supply or florists shops if you cannot locate them in the wild. The Pride of Madera grows along the coastal mountains of California.

The very fine seed tips on candy tuft and peppergrass weeds are some of the few natural growths small enough to be suitable for HO or larger-scale leaves. Some larger craft stores and florists' supply firms may carry the candy tuft or peppergrass during some seasons. An alternate is to use the etched brass leaves produced in HO or O scales by Scale Link in England (Figures 7-22 and 7-23).

Some types of pinecones can simulate small pine tree models of about 2 to 4 inches in height. The cones must have been lying on the ground long enough for birds and animals to have eaten the seeds, leaving only the hairlike inner core (see Figure 7-8). The cones need not be painted, but they must be covered with a light texture of fine-grind foam (Figure 7-17). Spray the foam and just the tips of the branches with an appropriate shade of green.

Do-It-Yourself Tree Building

Certainly, every tree assembled from a kit or from natural growths, ground polyurethane foam, or Woodland Scenics' Foliage Material is a do-it-yourself project. Some modelers, though, have created some clever and effective alternatives to tree construction. Jack Rice uses simple wooden meat skewers with clumps of foliage material and leftover foam to make conifers (Figure 7-18). The skewers are painted a bark color, and when the paint dries, they are dipped in undiluted artist's matte medium. Round clumps of stretched foliage material are pushed over the skewer and some loose ground foam sprinkled on before the matte medium dries.

Charles Bowdish uses 1/4- to 2-inch lengths of sisal rope, cut with scissors and unraveled into individual strands, to make the bristles or boughs on his bottle-brush trees (Figure 7-19). The trunk is steel wire, about 20

gauge, twisted into a rope with a hand drill. He clamps two strands of the wire in a vise, lays the boughs over the two wires, and twists the whole thing together. It's similar to the technique used to make the ready-made bottle-brush style pine trees sold by Faller, Life-Like, Heki, Kibri and Noch, except that the sisal produces a more random appearance. The boughs are then painted green and sprinkled with fine-grind foam for texture.

Fig. 7-16. Four materials for correct scale-size leaves: Scale Link etched brass leaves and twigs (left), ground foam (top), paper punches from a Telex machine (right), and Candy Tuft or Peppergrass weeds (bottom).

Fig. 7-17. Jack Rice painted pine cones gray/brown and textured them with fine-grind foam to simulate small firs on his HO scale layout. The shape is similar to the balsam fir.

Fig. 7-18. For nearly instant trees, Jack Rice uses Woodland Scenics' Foliage Material from the box with matching fine-grind foam to texture wooden meat skewers. The shapes are similar to the Douglas firs.

Fig. 7-19. Charles Bowdish and other modelers at the Buhl Planetarium use unraveled sisal rope fibers and fine steel wire to wind their own bottle-brush trees. Some fine-grind foam would improve the appearance. The shape is similar to the balsam fir.

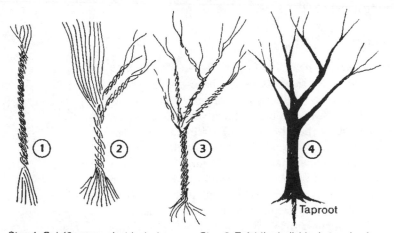

Fig. 7-20. The four steps in creating a root system, tree trunk, and limb structure from 10-gauge electrical wire or stranded clothesline cable.

Step 1: Cut 10-gauge electrical wire (insulation not shown) or stranded wire clothesline cable.

Step 2: Unravel portions of the upper ends for branches and twigs. Unravel the lower ends for root.

Step 3: Twist the individual strands of twig wires into branches.

Step 4: Texture the exposed root system, trunk, and branches with water putty.

THe Harvard Tree Museum

The most realistic tree models in the world are likely found in the middle of Massachusetts. The Fisher Museum of Forestry, at the 900-acre Harvard Forest, near Petersham, Mass., was completed in the late 1930s. The museum depicts the history of area forests with models that are approximately 1/12 scale but with forced perspective down to 1/200 scale.

Each of the trees in the museum's many dioramas was built by hand in the '20s and '30s. The tree limbs are twisted from wire, beginning with a series of loops. The results are similar to those in Figure 7-18, but the trunks are built from brass rod. Literally hundreds of dead trees, each with all the tiny twigs of a real tree, occupy the winter scenes. The summer scenes utilize the same twisted-wire technique, but each individual leaf is etched from brass and soldered to the tree twigs.

The leaves from Scale Link in Figures 7-22 and 7-23 are similar to those used by the builders of the museum in Harvard Forest. The Scale Link leaves, however, are already attached to the twigs in clusters of about 50 leaves—the builders at the Fisher Museum of Forestry added one leaf at a time! You can utilize their basic techniques, with the Scale Link 1/87 or 1/48 scale etched leaves, to create precise replicas of real trees in a fraction of the time. Most of us, though, will settle for a proper tree trunk and limbs shaped from wire, with some Woodland Scenics or AMSI Poly Fiber for twigs, and ground foam, in the proper leaf color, for the leaves.

Tree Trunk Construction

There is no suitable substitute for the dried roots of weeds (Figure 12-5), a real hedge clipping, sagebrush, or mesquite to simulate the trunk of a tree. These growths, however, can be used only to simulate certain species of tree. AMSI's or Woodland Scenics' cast-metal trunks can be used for most kinds of trees, but both brands have a limited selection of 4-inch or taller shapes. For larger trees or unusual shapes, or simply to save money, you will want to make some trunks for yourself. Figure 7-20 shows the four steps for building the root system, tree trunk, and branches for just about any size tree. Stranded clothesline cable or 10-gauge insulated electrical wire will produce a tree in the 4- to 8-inch range, depending on how rounded or oblong the shape. For larger trees, twist two or more pieces of wire or cable together in the main trunk area (Figure 7-21). This method allows you to model the often-visible upper roots of a tree. The root system also gives the tree extra support, and the taproot provides the peg for holding the tree while modeling it and planting it.

Tree Patterns for Modelers

The eighteen patterns in Figures 7-24 to 7-41 allow you to match most tree kits to the shape and texture of nearly any tree. The species shown are each only one example of the type of tree that has that shape and texture. Remember that the health and age of a tree can alter its appearance (Figures 7-42 and 7-43), so vary the shapes of all your trees. Use the darker lines in Figures 7-24 through 7-41 to shape cast-metal or wire trunks and limbs. The lightershaded areas must be shaped with macrame fibers, the similar Woodland Scenics Poly Fiber, or the mesh and foam foliage material from Woodland Scenics. The texture of the tree is achieved with either medium-grind (for some conifers with clumps of needles) or fine-grind foam. For variety, paper punchings that are left over when some banks cancel checks or the punchings from some older Telex machines can be dyed to simulate leaves and can be used as texture, or use the K&S Scenery Products or Noch Flakes. This technique is illustrated by Harry Sage's trees shown in the color section.

Individual Tree Leaves

If you use the twisted wire technique to build up the tree trunk, limbs, and fine twig structure, it is possible to create specific tree shapes. You can go a step further toward perfect realism by adding etched brass scale-size leaves that actually match the shape of that tree's species. The technique of using etched brass leaves on twisted wire tree trunks was pioneered by the Harvard Museum in Massachusetts. Scale Link in England offers a wide range of etched brass leaves and twigs in HO and O scales.

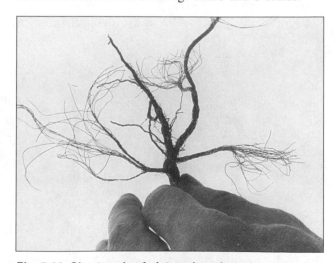

Fig. 7-21. Six strands of picture-hanging wire were used to make this tree form. The six are twisted together to form the trunk and two pairs of the wires are twisted together to make the two major vertical limbs, with single pieces of the wire to make the more horizontal limbs.

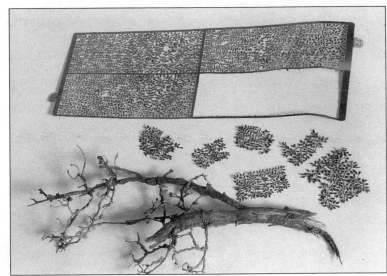

Fig. 7-22. A piece of sagebrush has been wrapped with small wires to create a twig structure (bottom). The Scale Link etched brass leaves (top) were painted green then cut from the sheet with a sharp knife into the six leave/twig pieces shown (center).

These Scale Link etched brass leaves are attached to a series of twigs so you can add about 50 leaves and their twigs at one time. The Broad Leaf etchings in Figures 7-22 and 7-23 can represent elm, beech, birch, black poplar, cherry, lime, and similar leaves. Scale Link also offers ash, maple, oak, chestnut, weeping willow, and a variety of palm and fern leaves. Spray the etchings an appropriate shade of green on one side and paint the bottoms of the leaves a shade or two lighter. Cut the leaf/twig sets from the etching with a sharp hobby knife or small diagonal cutters, and attach them to the ends of the tree twig wires with your choice of solder, thickened cyanoacrylate cement, or 5-minute epoxy. Touch-up the assembly points in the twig area with beige or gray paint. Twist the leaves

Fig. 7-23. Attach the etched brass twigs to the wire twigs on the tree with thickened cyanoacrylate cement, then bend the leaves into a natural shape so most leaves face the sun.

Fig. 7-24. Black cherry.

Fig. 7-25. White Oak.

Fig. 7-27. Gray birch.

into shape to match the real tree's outline. The leaves are the final element that can make a tree a truly accurate HO or O scale model. It's an expensive and time-consuming method of creating a tree, but the effect is incredible and well worth the effort and expense for foreground scenes or for just a tree or two in a diorama.

Palm Trees

The modeler has two choices if he needs palm trees for a diorama or model railroad; buy a Preiser kit (Figure 7-

44), a Plastruct or AMSI kit, or build palms using the techniques Willard Jones applied to his HO scale examples (Figure 7-45). The Preiser kits are fine if the species and size (about 9 inches) are suitable. To duplicate Willard Jones's balsa wood palms, scrape a wood saw blade along the soft balsa. For rough, scale-like palm bark, wrap

Fig. 7-26. American Elm.

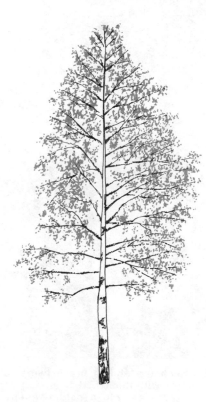

Fig. 7-28. Quaking aspen.

Fig. 7-29. Weeping willow.

Fig. 7-31. Maple.

Fig. 7-30. Lombardy poplar.

Fig. 7-32. Copper beech.

Fig. 7-33. Ash.

Fig. 7-35. Balsam fir.

Fig. 7-34. Sycamore.

Fig. 7-36.Mature Douglas fir.

Fig. 7-37. Young Douglas fir.

Fig. 7-39. White pine.

Fig. 7-38. Red pine.

Fig. 7-40. White spruce

Campbell's HO scale paper roof shingles around the tree. The dead palm fronds and seeds can be simulated with white wool or synthetic macrame twine dyed the proper color (see Reference Card 18). Unravel it and glue it to the trunk with artist's matte medium. The actual palm fronds are green-colored feathers, available at craft supply stores. Weather the fronds with some beige to tone down their bright green hues (see Reference Card 17).

Planting Trees

No miniature tree is complete until it is planted in the diorama. Figure 7-43 shows how the site for each tree can affect its growth. Of course, you must make adjustments in the normal pattern of twigs, leaves, or needles when you build the trees for special locations. Trees do not always grow straight out of the ground, but the effect of nearly any leaning tree is not realistic in a miniature scene. Except for some dead or dying trees, all model trees must be positioned to stand straight. The pin that protrudes from the bottom of the trunk will secure the tree, but you may have to mix a small batch of molding plaster, plaster of paris, or even water putty with some color to pack around the base of the trunk. The plaster will hold the tree upright, and you can shape and carve the plaster to simulate exposed roots. If you don't want to bother with modeling roots, cover the base of the tree with

Fig. 7-41. Black spruce.

Stage 1: Young tree; full growth, partial symmetry, barely visible root system.

Stage 2: Mature trees; dead branches, gaps in foliage, more exposed root system.

Stage 3: Older tree: Needles near branch tips, large bare areas, even more exposed root system.

Fig. 7-42. A typical conifer during the basic stages of its life cycle.

A. Sparse needles on windward side.
B. Sparse needles near the center of the grove.
C. Sparse needles near rock cliffs.

Fig. 7-43. The effect of weather and adjacent cliffs on the foliage of conifers. The effect on deciduous trees is similar.

Fig. 7-44. Preiser palm tree kits are all plastic. The completed tree is shown at left.

Fig. 7-45. Willard Jones made these towering palms using balsa trunks, twine leaf shards, and feathers.

dirt or brown ground foam and hold it in place with bonding agent. Grass seldom grows around the roots of trees, but you may want to use some yellow-gray ground foam or paper punchings to simulate fallen leaves. Don't forget, as most modelers do, that nearly all stands of mature trees are surrounded by a few fresh saplings. And remember that it is rare for a single tree to grow in the wild. There are usually at least three trees in a grove.

Forests

Few modelers attempt to duplicate dense forests, but the technique can be accomplished nearly as quickly as covering the same surface area with any other texture. For a dense forest, model two or three rows of complete trees and trunks along the outer edges of the forest (Figure 7-46). Bring the plaster hillside upward behind these first rows of trees and plant the upper halves of all remaining trees. Before planting the inner groves, paint the plaster dark brown to simulate the floor of a shaded forest. Obviously, this technique demands some preplanning of the shape of the plaster scenery. If you use the Hydrocal and paper-towel technique for hillsides that is described in Chapter 4, you can build up the hillside with wadded-up newspapers and cover them with the Hydrocal-soaked paper towels. You might also want to include a rock casting or two (see Chapter 4) to simulate exposed boulders or cliffs above the tops of the trees. You can also use Woodland Scenics' Poly Fiber or AMSI's mesh for the interior of the forest and surround it with complete tree models as shown in the color section.

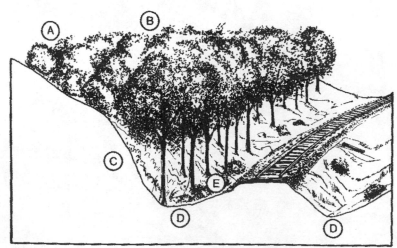

A. Smaller treetops of finer texture.
B. Treetops of similar size and texture; these imply "whole" trees, even where no trunks exist.
C. Slope angles uphill to disguise the lack of trunks on the back rows of trees.
D. Drainage ditches.
E. Undergrowth.

Fig. 7-46. A cutaway view showing how a dense forest can be simulated with just a few completed trees on the edges. Twig and foliage textures without trunks make up the rest of the forest. See photo in the color section.

CHAPTER 8

Water and Seascapes

There is no more visually exciting miniature scenic effect than water. State-of-the-art has a double meaning when applied to the simulation of water in miniature. Two nearly odor-free products, epoxy and artist's gloss medium, produce crystal-clear, sturdy surfaces that look so much like water you have to touch them to believe they are not real. The pioneer model makers' search for ways to make realistic-looking water have at last been rewarded with materials that, for the modeler, truly are better than water.

Beginning at the Bottom

Epoxy and artist's gloss medium have one thing in common with real water. They run like water while they are still fluid. This means that they will spread perfectly level. Both will flow through even a pinhole-size gap in the plaster scenery, but the problems of self-leveling and leaking will not be critical on small streams or rapids where the simulated water is brushed on. Small ponds, wide streams, lakes, or harbors *must* be prepared for the

Fig. 8-1. Partially submerged logs are enclosed in the last three or four 1/8-inch thick pours of epoxy to make a simulated logging pond.

99

Fig. 8-2. Create small streams on top of finished scenery (including this, made with the "Grass-That-Grows" felt and dirt system from Chapter 6) by gluing small pebbles to the bottom of the valley with artist's matte medium. Simulate the water with artist's gloss medium poured directly into the streambed.

epoxy or gloss medium by completely sealing the plaster surface. Perhaps the best sealer is full-strength latex interior wall paint in an appropriate earth shade, with enough white or toner mixed in to match the surrounding soil or dirt. Never sift any loose foam, real dirt, or any other loose texture onto the bottom of any watercourse. Air bubbles become trapped and are visible, particularly when epoxy cures and hardens. The air bubbles look like submerged diamonds, and they permanently destroy the realism of the

scene. The problem is not quite so acute with artist's gloss medium, but artist's gloss is not effective for model water that is more than about 1/4-inch deep. Mask off the stream area while you texture the surrounding surfaces and, to be safe, vacuum the bottom of any watercourse just before you pour in the epoxy or gloss medium.

Streams and Ponds

Just about any shiny or clear glossy paint could be used to simulate small streams and ponds. But most of these paints have an offensive odor and are difficult to clean up. Artist's gloss medium dries glossy and almost clear (Figure 8-2). Because it has a water base, it is less likely to discolor the bottom of the watercourse. Use a good quality brush or an eye dropper to apply the gloss medium exactly where you want it. The easiest way to simulate ponds is to pour the gloss medium into the depression that will form the pond. Continue pouring until the edges of the pond have filled the intended area. You'll achieve a perfectly natural meandering shoreline with this method and be assured that the surface will be level. The gloss medium is thick enough to brush up some small peaks which will dry to form natural ripples on the surface. The pouring technique can also be used to create natural small streams. However, this method is risky because you may find that the pockets and hollows of the stream become just a series of ponds. Small streams can be simulated far more effectively and with

Fig. 8-3. Mix Envirotex in old cans or paper cups. A fresh cup should be used for each pour.

Fig. 8-4. A light bulb can be held near the epoxy to speed up curing time and help create gentle ripples in the hardened surface. Do not allow the hot bulb to touch the surface of the "water."

more control by brushing the gloss medium exactly where you *hope* the stream will flow.

Using Decoupage Epoxy for Water

The decoupage craft has been responsible for the creation of several different types of plastic materials that dry crystal clear and with a hard surface. Recently, these compounds have been improved so that virtually no undesirable odor is produced as the material cures from its liquid to a solid state. The better-known brands are Envirotex Lite and UltraGlo 1:1 Polymer Coating, a special two-part epoxy that has little odor. It differs from the resins recommended in some publications because the hardener fluid (or catalyst) is mixed in a 1:1 ratio with the resin. The previous materials were mixed with just a few drops of hardener to a cup of resin and produce an unpleasant, if not unhealthy, odor. New epoxies seem to have all the advantages of the older resins without the disadvantages. Mix the decoupage hardener and resin thoroughly and in equal parts. You may want to add a drop or two of special resin dye (the type used in casting resins) to the mixture to duplicate special water conditions. Never use a conventional two-part epoxy, which is too thick to provide a level water-like flow. Always wear latex gloves and eye protection when working with any resin or epoxy.

There is no particular limit to the surface area you can cover with a single pouring of Envirotex Lite or Ultra-

Glo. However, limit the *depth* of each pour to 1/8 inch or less to avoid cracking. If you mix too much, pour it into another watercourse before it cures. Heat speeds the curing process, so you might want to hold a light bulb near the water surface until it cures (Figure 8-4). Work in a room that is fairly warm, at least 70 degrees. In a cooler room, keep a light bulb or two burning near the water. The fluid cures with just the faintest hint of a ripple on the surface, which is too calm for any scale-model pond or lake. With a wooden tongue depressor or ice-cream stick, poke at the surface just as the resin begins to cure or set; the pockets will *almost* smooth over to form gentle ripples in the surface. If the lake, river, or harbor is supposed to be more than about 2 inches deep, reduce its depth by pouring pre-colored molding plaster or plaster of paris into the valley. Color the plaster to match the surrounding areas, but mix it to the consistency of thick cream so that it will be self-leveling. Stop pouring the plaster when the level is within the 2-inch minimum of what will later be the top surface of the decoupage epoxy water.

Coloring Envirotex Lite or Ultra-Glo

If you are creating a lake or harbor with 1-1/2 to 2 inches of epoxy, add enough navy blue dye to the mixture to make the plaster lake or harbor bottom virtually invisible after the first 1/8-inch-thick pouring of epoxy. Add just a trace of the dye to the next few pours and no dye at all to the last pour or two. You will discover that you can sim-

101

ulate very deep water with as little as 1/2 inch of Enviro-tex Lite or Ultra-Glo using this dye technique. You can skip the first dye by pouring the flat plaster bottom, then spraying the flat surface with dark blue-green paint. Allow the plaster and paint to dry for at least a week before pouring the epoxy. With this technique, all of the depth of the lake or harbor except the last 1/2 inch is actually plaster. This technique makes it far easier to submerge docks, piers, logs, sunken ships, and other bottom debris because the plaster will hold the debris exactly where you want it for the later pourings. You can often rest boat bottoms on this plaster or partially embed the keel of the boat in it to hold the items firmly when the water is added.

The Shoreline

Artist's gloss medium and the resins like Envirotex Lite and Ultra-Glo have nearly opposite characteristics at the places where the wet material ends and the dry shore begins. The gloss medium is so thick that the surface of

the water may actually be higher than the shore. The solution here is to brush the gloss medium along the shore-line with a paint brush, a wooden tongue depressor, or an ice-cream stick. The epoxy will pull itself up into the shoreline to produce a concave water edge. Wait until it hardens completely, then paint the shoreline with latex or Polly Scale paint, and, if you wish, sprinkle on some dirt, ground foam, or other texture material. If you plan to have weeds or bushes growing in the shallow water's edge, insert them into the last 1/8-inch pour of epoxy or into the surface of the gloss medium before either fluid hardens.

Rapids, Waterfalls, and Other White Water

Artist's gloss medium is thick enough to be brushed over a slope as steep as about 45 degrees and to a thickness of nearly 1/16 inch before it will run. You will have to experiment to determine just how much of a slope you can paint with the gloss medium, but remember that you can go back with more coats to build up the depth. In general, you

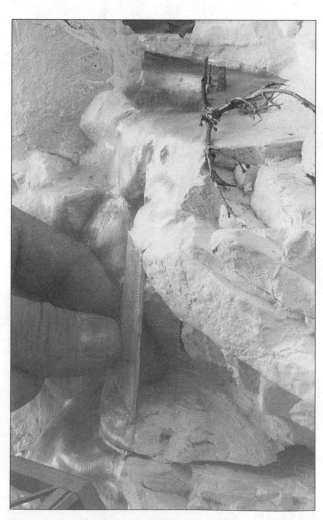

Fig. 8-5. This Color-Rite plastic waterfall uses fluffed cotton to simulate spray at the bottom of each fall. Cellophane and gloss medium instead of cotton may also be used.

Fig. 8-6. Thick slabs of artist's gloss medium, colored with streaks of white and pearl, are glued to the sides of rocks to simulate falls.

will discover that if water would actually flow over the simulated rock bed of your rapid-flowing stream, the gloss medium will duplicate that effect. If the slope is so steep that a waterfall would form, you will have to build that portion of the rapids and install it *before* pouring or brushing on the actual stream. When the gloss medium has dried completely, brush on the faintest trace of pearl-colored fingernail polish to simulate frothing white water. Simulate the texture of the bubbling water by pocking and stirring the gloss medium just as it sets. If you want a large mass of bubbling water, such as at the foot of a waterfall, crumple up cellophane, pin it in place with straight pins (but leave the heads sticking up 1/4 inch), and pour gloss medium over the cellophane. When the first layer dries, pull the pins out and add another layer of gloss medium. Finally, add touches of pearl fingernail polish.

The simplest way to create a waterfall is to use the Color-Rite kit made of plastic that can be cut to any length or width (Figure 8-5). For smaller waterfalls, paint three to six layers of gloss medium onto a clean plate of glass.

Fig. 8-7. To simulate large expanses of water, use a sheet of plywood or polyfoam insulation board for the surface. Apply a 1/8-inch thick layer of texture paint to the surface of the board. Use a textured sponge roller or a long-haired brush-style roller to dab at the surface—do not roll it—to pull the texture paint into peaks as shown. Practice the technique to get a pattern for the peaks that matches that of the real water you are modeling.

Fig. 8-8. The peaks formed with the texture paint will soften into replicas of small waves as the paste dries. Paint the surface of the "water" a dark green to match photographs of the water you are modeling. Polly Scale "Grimy Black" is often a place to start to find a matching color. When the paint is dry, coat the surface with a clear scratch-resistant varnish like Varathane to provide the" wet" look.

Fig. 8-9. The waves on Tom Knapp's N scale model of a California beach were shaped in plaster of paris and painted blue-green and white.

When the gloss medium dries, scrape it from the glass with a single-edge razor blade. Cut the material into strips and brush on a thin series of white flow lines with Polly Scale paints. Cover the Polly Scale with another coat of gloss medium *after* you have glued the simulated water-falls or rivulets into the streambed with gloss medium (Figure 8-6). Add a few light streaks of pearl fingernail polish after the last coat of gloss medium is dry.

Seascapes

The oceans, seas, and Great Lakes are some of the most difficult portions of the real world to bring down to a miniature scene with any degree of realism. One of the major problems with such large bodies of water is that the horizon is nearly impossible to duplicate because of the unlimited variety of viewing positions available to anyone admiring your model. Movie and television special-effects experts can make a credible ocean from a swimming-pool sized body of water because they control the horizon by controlling the camera angle. The modeler, however, must be prepared to slice through the ocean along at least one side of any scene and hope that the boat or shoreline will distract the viewer away from the missing horizon. Nevertheless, the seascape-building technique is well worth developing, since most miniature ships look more realistic resting in an ocean or harbor diorama.

Fig. 8-10. Dave Simpson's 12 x 12-inch diorama of a scratch-built N scale railroad car ferry has epoxy "water" complete with bow waves and wake.

You can learn from the mistakes of generations of modelers and not model any water effects that are deeper than about two inches. Real water becomes murky at that depth. The trick is to include enough dye in the lower depths of the water so that the bottom appears to be some indefinable depth below the visible depth. A depth of just one inch of simulated water is enough to convey the feeling. To avoid cutting the hull of a full-hull model ship make the water deeper by pouring plastic water up to the ship's waterline. In some cases, you might want to extend partially submerged ships, anchor lines, or broken piers as far as two inches below the surface. If you must have deep water, the best technique for creating it involves two materials: one to build up the depth to the *lowest* ebb point of any waves, and the second to mold and shape the waves.

To use decoupage epoxy for deep water where the edge of the table, diorama, or benchwork cuts through the water, you must build a temporary water-tight dam to create the vertical edge for the epoxy water. Six to ten layers of plastic Baggies can be sandwiched between the baseboard for the diorama or the edge of the model railroad benchwork and a piece of perfectly flat plywood. The extra layers of Baggies should provide plenty of sealing surface to prevent the fluid epoxy from running out. Be sure to stretch the Baggies tight and flat so they won't be captured inside the resin. You can spray their surface with a light spray of silicone lubricant, which acts as a mold release. The Baggies can be pulled away from the hardened vertical edge of the resin. Mix only enough resin to form a layer between 1/8- and 1/4-inch thick and allow that layer to harden for 48 hours before pouring in the next 1/8- to 1/4-inch layer. Repeat the pours and the 48-hour setting periods between each pour until the resin is as deep as you desire.

If you cannot look directly down into the "water" you are modeling, it is possible to simulate large rivers, lakes

Fig. 8-11. The harbor on Willard Jones' HO scale railroad has clear epoxy "water" with a removable freight-car-carrying barge.

and even oceans with a flat board for the surface of the water. Use a wide putty knife to scoop the still-wet paste into the peaks of waves. Try to make the peaks as sharp as you can because they will soften considerably as the paste dries. Practice the technique to get a pattern for the peaks that matches that of the real water you are modeling. Most deep water is a dark shade of green that is similar to the Polly Scale "Grimy Black." You may want to mix a bit of white paint with the Grimy Black color or, perhaps, add a bit more green or blue to match the color of the photograph of the real water you are modeling. When the paint is dry, coat the surface with a clear scratch-resistant varnish like Varathane to provide the "wet" look.

Boat and Ship Scenes

A diorama with a ship or boat cutting through the simulated water with a series of bow waves and a frothy wake is exciting to see in pictures, but it is seldom realistic in model form. You expect those waves to be frozen in a photograph, but you also expect them to be moving when you see them in three dimensions, even as a model diorama. This same logic applies to rolling breakers or waves like those in Tom Knapp's N scale harbor scene (Figure 8-9 and the color section). For maximum realism, limit your dioramas with ships to harbor scenes or even dry dock scenes where the lack of water action is not noticeable.

For that dramatic water-in-motion effect, you have two choices: Mold the actual waves in plaster, as Tom Knapp did, or use several layers of artist's gloss gel on top of the resin depths to build up the shapes you desire. The gloss gel is thick enough to form as much as 1/4-inch high wave peaks while it is still wet. With four or five applications, you can create just about any bow wave or wake froth effect (Figure 8-10). If you mold the waves in plaster, brush on three or four coats of artist's gloss medium to give a water-like gloss and depth. The major difference between the two processes is that you can dye the lower layers of resin to create more realistic depths to the water, whereas using plaster waves demands that you color the plaster surface alone. Use the same techniques for creating rapids and other white water.

The Beach

The frothy water washed ashore by waves helps to hide the actual bottom of any beach. This means that you have the freedom either to model the beach bottom to where the ocean is an inch or so deep and pour in the En-

virotex or to shape the ocean in plaster using the artist's gloss medium techniques. Simulated sand or rocks must be applied before the final coat of resin or gloss medium. Do not run sifted sand so far into the water that the resin can cover it, since air bubbles probably will appear. To be safe, model the shape of the beach in Hydrocal or plaster and paint it the proper color. You can also add any rocks or stones larger than about 1/4 inch. Then pour in the resin until it reaches to within 1/16 inch of the *depth of* the water on the shore. Now you can apply the sand using the same techniques for applying real dirt described in Chapter 6. Sift the sand through a tea strainer, then through a number 100-sieve brass plumber's screen, and use only the particles that pass through the tea strainer but not through the 100sieve. When the bonding agent that holds the sand dries, apply the final 1/16 inch of *depth* using artist's gloss medium.

The Harbor

Harbors are usually full of activity in real life, and these activities can be modeled with a high degree of credibility. A viewer expects some pause in any work activity, so a frozen-in-time diorama or model-railroad harbor scene will be more realistic than one where the boats or ships are *supposed to be* moving. The most important element of the harbor scene is just what you hope it will be—your ship models. When you create a diorama with the ship moving through choppy seas or kicking up a bow wave, the viewer's attention is focused more on the water than on the diorama. The harbor scene allows use of the proven theatrical techniques in Chapters 1 and 9, as well as most of the chapters that follow.

For the model railroader, the harbor can be a perfect source of freight shipments of almost any kind. The car ferry (Figures 8-10 and 8-11), another harbor-based industry, can provide for the shipment of a half-dozen model freight cars carrying a great variety of products. Stone walls and pilings are typical scenery for harbors. The pilings can be simple wooden dowels with extra grain scraped into them with the blade of a razor saw. For simulated barnacles, attach some fine-grind foam with artist's matte medium, and color it a seaweed gray-green. Mr. Plaster has cast plaster pilings, in N and HO scales, that are painted and textured with barnacles. Remember, too, that harbors appear on large rivers, long lakes, the Great Lakes, and in river deltas, as well as on oceans. A barge scene would be equally suitable in a scene that depicts New Jersey, Missouri, British Columbia, Alaska, and a host of other locations.

CHAPTER 9

Close-Up Credibility and Superdetails

Perhaps the best definition of superdetails is the "greatly overlooked obvious." For example, you cannot build a realistic model of a modern interstate highway without including tar-filled cracks and paper debris along the roadside. Similarly, no forest scene is complete without fallen branches. A superdetail falls into the general category of debris. If you train yourself to look at a real life scene or a photograph of a historical scene and pick out the debris, you will begin to develop the skill that makes any model scene into a realistic work of art. Debris usually is not considered pretty enough to be included in a model, but any model scene that lacks debris lacks the most important *living* element of any real-life scene.

Basic Clutter

The clutter that surrounds a scene *defines the* scene. You won't find many fallen tree limbs beneath trees in a park; the freshly mown grass is what defines the scene as a park. Fallen tree limbs, dead leaves, and a random array

Fig. 9-1. Bob Brown's O scale engine house captures the look of a backwoods branch-line operation.

107

Fig. 9-2. George DeWolfe's 1/35 scale diorama depicts a peasant's hut.

of weeds, grasses, and general ground contours define a natural setting, the *opposite* of a park scene. The wooden washtub, rough-hewn pitchfork, and rope-trussed bird define the log hut as that of a peasant in George DeWolfe's diorama (Figure 9-2). The piles of wheels, gears, and other mechanical clutter define Bob Brown's narrow-gauge engine house (Figure 9-1) as a backwoods scene. Bob's 1/4-inch scale scenes were among the earlier dioramas to emphasize the importance of clutter as well as weathering. Clutter can date the scene; fresh concrete suggests a new highway, while jagged tar strips and roughened textures suggest aged concrete. A street scene with only sidewalks has no life until parking meters, mailboxes, awnings, streetlights, lights for signs, curbs, gutters, drains, manholes, and fire hydrants are added. Re-creating any scene in miniature will force you to see clutter you never noticed before, and adding that clutter will give the scene a true-to-life effect.

Handmade Debris and Litter

In the previous chapters, warnings have been given about the unnatural appearance of dyed sawdust, real rocks, and untreated lichen. The clutter suggested in this chapter is really just another form of *texture*. Clutter, debris, and litter provide evidence of human activity. With the exceptions of parks and new highways, every other portion of the scenes we model will likely be covered with dead limbs, natural erosion, naturally broken and man-cut tree stumps, old fences and other discarded scraps of lumber, tangles of barbed wire or old cable, empty cans and barrels, and so on. The modeler is blessed with an incredible array of commercial products to make it easier to duplicate debris texture, but most debris can be made from things around the house, including the fine twig ends of hedges and weeds, nylon sewing thread, broken wooden matches, pieces of wooden toothpicks and meat skewers (to represent cans and short pieces of pipe), leftover bits of wood or plastic from any kit, crumpled bits of aluminum foil, and foil pressed over a coarse metal file (to make corrugations like those near the upper center of Figure 9-1), and bits of facial tissue folded and painted to simulate tarps or empty cloth sacks. In addition to the usual earth textures, you will want to add small piles and spills of coal, sand, and railroad track ballast. Firms like Campbell, Faller, Highball, Life-Like, Plastruct, Rock Quarry, Smith & Sons, Vollmer, and Woodland Scenics make all three of these textures in a variety of sizes and colors. You can also use real coal, sand, or ballast that has been crushed with a hammer inside a cloth bag and sifted through a 40-sieve size tea strainer.

Off-the-Shelf Clutter and Debris

The Walthers' *HO Railroad Catalog* and JMC International's *Source Book* contain hundreds of scale-size metal castings for details like electrical meters, parking meters, hand tools, buckets, cans, barrels, industrial wheels, gears, and pulleys, downspouts, pipe and pipe fittings, and just about anything else you might find in a hardware store. All of these are suitable for models between about 1/160 and 1/40 scale. There is also a wide selection of different sizes of chain, hooks, and, from Vintage Reproductions, even scale-size cable. Don't forget scale-size railroad spikes, short lengths of rail or structural angle iron and I-beams, tie plates, rail joiners, and scale nuts and bolts, all listed in the Walthers and JMC catalogs. These items are suitable for military dioramas as well as for railroad, dock, or other industrial scenes. Military modelers will want to watch for the boxes of plastic parts and clutter in 1/76, 1/48, and 1/35 scales from the same firms that make tanks and other armored vehicles. Railroad modelers, especially those working in S or O scales, should take a good look at these military diorama details; there are some real bargains in details, such as barrels, tools, wheels, tires, fences, and even scale-model people.

Chooch and Mr. Plaster produce what must be the ultimate in easy-to-use debris or clutter texture—one-piece precolored and weathered moldings of entire piles of junk (Figure 9-3). Chooch offers loads of scrap and junk for Athearn and Roundhouse 40- and 50-foot gondolas. These can be used as-is for piles of junk around any industrial scene in just about any scale. The firm also has assorted junk piles in both HO (1/87) scale (Figure 13-5, left) and O (1/48) scale. The piles of junk can be cut apart to produce six various-sized individual piles. Use a coping saw or a jeweler's saw to cut the castings. The 40- and 50-foot HO scale gondola loads can also be cut into several shorter piles. When you install this debris in the scenery, mask it carefully until the surrounding dirt and ground foam is in place and the bonding agent has dried. You can sift on more loose dirt and green foam to simulate weeds and add some foxtail or cattail weeds (see Figures 6-8 and 6-10) to add incredible realism to the Chooch or Mr. Plaster castings.

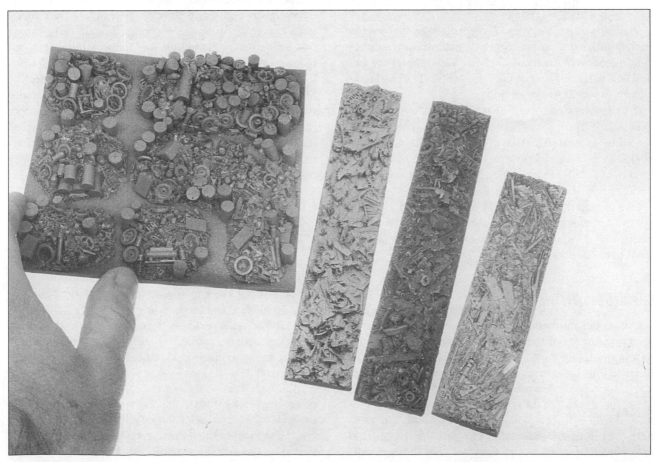

Fig. 9-3. Chooch's HO scale "Piles of Junk" (left) and loads of junk and scrap for HO scale gondolas (right) are pre-painted epoxy castings.

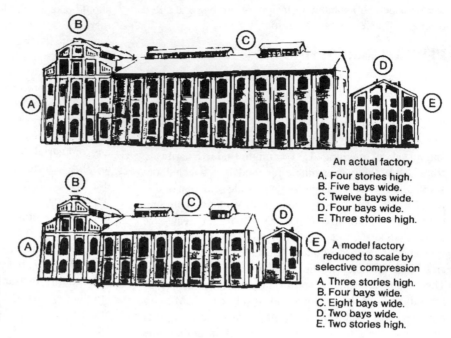

An actual factory
A. Four stories high.
B. Five bays wide.
C. Twelve bays wide.
D. Four bays wide.
E. Three stories high.

A model factory reduced to scale by selective compression
A. Three stories high.
B. Four bays wide.
C. Eight bays wide.
D. Two bays wide.
E. Two stories high.

Fig. 9-4. The technique of selective compression reduces the size of a real structure while retaining its proportions and scale-size windows and doors.

Buildings as Scenery

Before you create your own scene, take the time to study similar real-world scenes so that you can identify what elements of the scene, such as building height or texture or a balance between tall and short and old and new, make real-world scenes exciting.

Nearly every real world structure offers some outside evidence of its function. These finer details were once reserved for contest models, but today many of them are included even in inexpensive plastic kits. Some of the most important details are the evidence of that structure's links with the rest of the world. Be sure to include at least one source of electrical power in the form of a nearby pole, if not the actual wires leading to the insulator on the structure itself. Be sure also that some type of path or road leads to every door.

Selective Compression

No model railroader is foolish enough to attempt to re-create any more than a tiny fraction of a real mountain in miniature. Even if reduced to N (1/160) scale, a relatively low 500-foot hill would soar nearly 3 feet above the table. Wise modelers duplicate the proper angle of the slopes and the correct scale textures and reproduce nearly full-size trees in the foreground. The trees near the top of the mountains and near the background are reduced in size, getting ever smaller as they get closer to the crest of the hill or the backdrop in a forced

perspective. This same principle can be applied when reducing any real-world structure to a suitable size for a model railroad. With the exception of relatively small one- or two-story buildings, *any* large building can be reduced to help conserve space without noticeably affecting its proportions. Figure 9-4 shows how the Holly Sugar Plant in Santa Ana, Calif., can be reduced by half for a full-scale model. Selective compression does not reduce the size of doors or windows; it merely reduces the building's overall pro*portions*. The building retains its character even in reduced scale. The technique can be used for bridges as well.

A Firm Foundation

The most glaring flaw in most model buildings is the dark, shadowed gap between the foundation and the earth or pavement that surrounds it. The model looks as though it had been dropped in place by some giant (which of course it was). The gap around the base of any building must be hidden, and the building must rest in the scene with all four walls perfectly horizontal. Many otherwise-realistic scenes are spoiled by buildings that tilt and lean at right angles to the ground rather than at right angles to the *horizon*.

Buildings must be planned *before* the scenery is in place. Use blocks of wood or scraps of cardboard to mount the building supports so that they are secure and perfectly level. Use a carpenter's bubble-type level *every* time to be sure. You can then drape plaster or Hydrocal scenery everywhere but directly on the building site. Avoid any chance of getting the hills too close by tracing a bright red outline of the building with a grease pencil. Stop the plaster application when you're within 1/8 inch or so of the building outline. The building can be buried with an additional application of plaster or by installing the building before you install the ground-cover textures; these textures will fill in any gaps around the base. If you want to avoid trapping the structure in plaster and bonding agent, coat the base of the building with Micro-Scale Micro Mask, a liquid mask that can be peeled off when dry, and apply a touch of Vaseline over it. When the texturing is completely dry, remove the building, peel off the mask, and replace the building. The techniques for planting the abutments and lowest beams of bridges in Chapter 3 will work just as well with mines and other structures on pilings.

The City as Scenery

Too few modelers consider urban scenes worth re-creating. The city, however, provides one of the most practical means of camouflaging the necessary disappearance of the tracks on most model railroads. Trains can simply disappear behind buildings without the need to make excuses for too many tunnels. Hills and mountains consume a considerable amount of scarce table space because of their slopes; it takes at least a foot of table space for every foot of elevation on a realistic mountain slope. The result of this hillside problem is that modelers use too many rock cliffs on their railroads. City buildings rise vertically, with the only necessary ground space being the streets, curbs, and loading docks. The most effective use of the city as scenery is on the HO scale model railroad of the Sverna Park Model Railroad Club near Baltimore, Md. Dr. Logan Holtgrewe and the other club members have created a city scene that uses every trick, from selective compression to flats to cutout portions of calendar photos as flats. The entire city occupies only about 4 x 12 feet. About 4 x 6 feet of it is visible in Figures 9-5 and 9-6, about the same as most average size model railroads. Dr. Holtgrewe built most of the buildings from scratch, but there are nearly a hundred HO scale structure kits that could be used to duplicate the effect.

Fig. 9-5. Dr. Logan Holtgrewe scratch-built the foreground buildings and used cutout color photographs of real structures as flats on this Sverna Park Model Railroad Club layout.

Fig. 9-6. A bird's eye view of the Sverna Park city scene reveals that nearly all the buildings are flats. A few water tanks and chimneys suggest roofs.

Fig. 9-7. Most of the figures in this city scene, created by Magnuson Models to display its structures, are in static poses.

Fig. 9-8. The bases of the figures in Magnuson's city scene have been removed and pins stuck into the legs and platform to support them.

Buildings as Flats

The relatively high level of the track (about 48 inches from the floor) allows the structures in the Sverna Park city scene to reach *above the* eye level of even the tallest spectator. This means that there is no need to consider a horizon (see Chapter 10) and, more important, that only the fronts of the buildings are visible. Because the structures are placed close together, as in any real city, the view of the sides is blocked by adjacent buildings. The roofs are not visible because they stretch above eye level. The net result is that most of the structures need to be modeled only as fronts or flats (Figures 9-5 and 9-6). If you use kits for the structures, only one wall has to be supported; the ends and back wall can be located elsewhere or joined to the front wall to increase the length or height of the structure. The bird's-eye view of the Sverna Park scene in Figure 9-6 reveals that little layout space is occupied by the buildings; most of the benchwork is covered with tracks hidden by the flats but accessible by reaching over the tops of the flats. The technique allows you to fill a large area with structures with no more effort or time than filling the same area with hills or mountains.

People and Animals

Diorama builders usually prefer to have people in active poses, whereas model railroaders can create more realistic scenes with people in static or resting poses: sitting, leaning, or just standing. There are two obvious differences in these approaches. The proponents of active poses feel they are creating a frozen moment in history. The true essence of most military modelers' dioramas is this stop-action effect, but the effect does not work as well in three dimensions as it does in two. A scene where you cannot tell whether the figures are frozen in action or simply resting is the most enjoyable to view. In any case, the resting poses are far easier to make realistic. Action poses usually work for museum modelers, but most of us are amateurs and lack the skills and experience of the pros.

Modifying Ready-Made People

Most HO (1/87) and O (1/48) scale cast metal and molded plastic people and animals have a built-in or glued-on base to keep them upright. The first step in making them realistic is to remove a molded-on base with a razor saw. If the base is glued on, you can probably dissolve the glue joint with a half-dozen applications of liquid cement for plastics. When the base is free, allow the cement to dry for about a week because it may have softened the plastic. To support the figures, insert a straight pin through the bottom of the foot (or hoof or paw). Use a number 70-size drill bit in a pin vise and drill a hole. When the pin is in place, cut off the head with a pair of diagonal cutters so that about 1/8 to 1/4 inch protrudes from the figure. This length can usually be pushed directly into wooden platforms and plaster scenery, but you may also have to drill the pin hole in Hydrocal, plastic, or metal surfaces. The pin will hold the figure upright, but it is flexible enough to bend it slightly. In most scenes, the figures can be removed from their pinholes, which are not noticeable enough to detract from the scene. All of the model figures, from N-scale workmen to the 1/35 scale plastic infantrymen, have truly incredible details and relief, from the faces to the clothing with its tucks and folds. When these figures are painted, though, they somehow lose much of their three-dimensional effect. The solution is simple. Add extra shadow detail to the recesses and touch a bit of lighter color to the high spots to give them highlights. When you mix the paints for the face, for example, drop some of the paint onto a piece of glass with an eye dropper. Add a small puddle of a darker matching color and a small puddle of off-white (Figure 9-10). Paint the face with skin color (Reference Card 23). While the paint is still wet, use a number 0000 brush or a brush with just two or three bristles to add darker tones to the recessed areas around the eyes and neck and lighter tones to raised areas like cheekbones. For 1/48 scale or larger figures, paint the eyes first; for smaller-scale figures, paint the eyes after the flesh tones dry. Use a wash of brown to highlight the mouth. When painting a dozen or more figures, use the three-step technique on Reference Card 23 to

speed up the process. The key to this technique is to highlight the shading and molded-in details on the figure when a wash of a darker tone is applied. The wash will blend nicely into the recesses while running clear of any raised areas. A nearly dry brush-tip touch of a lighter color will provide a similarly quick highlight for cheeks and other raised areas. For well-worn clothing on military figures or construction crews, add Steps 4 and 5 of the weathering technique on Reference Card 25.

People, as well as domestic and farm animals, are available pre-painted in N, HO, and O scales from Bachmann, Dyna-Models, LaBelle, Model Power, IHC, NJ, Noch, Mini-Metal, Kibri, Merten, and Preiser. Durango Press, Lytler & Lytler, Atlas, LaBelle, MDK, and Preiser offer unpainted figures. The Walthers and JMC International catalogs illustrate most of the figures available in the smaller scales. In many military vehicle sets, 1/48 and 1/35 scale figures are included or sold as accessory packs. Few of the painted figures are done with enough neatness to be realistic. Most painted figures should be touched up with washes to accent their colors and a coat of Testor's DullCote applied to kill the glossy paint. The pre-painted animals are more acceptable than most pre-painted human figures. However, nearly all of the animals can benefit from a dry-brushing coat of a slightly darker shade to emphasize the textures of hair. The dry-brushing technique requires that you barely touch the extreme ends of the brush bristles to the paint. The paint is then dabbed onto the model with very light strokes to produce hair-like streaks of colors. For highlighting humans and clothing, the dry-brush technique is altered to produce a dabbing on-off stroke with the tip of the brush. A final wash of 19 parts water to 1 part Polly Scale Roof Brown (with 4 drops of dishwashing detergent added per pint of fluid) will help to accent the molded-in detail on any animal figure.

Fig. 9-9. These Preiser HO scale figures have been repainted to make them the focal point of a foreground scene in Magnuson's diorama.

Fig. 9-10. Mix lighter and darker shades on a glass palette (left) and blend shadow and highlights directly on the figure with a number 0000 paintbrush.

CHAPTER 10

Backdrops, Perspective, and Lighting

The primary purpose of a backdrop behind a model railroad or diorama is to convey the feeling that the scene extends to the horizon and beyond. The single most important element is the horizon because that is where our eye tells us the scene ends. No large diorama and no model railroad scene will be credible without a horizon positioned at or above the eye level of the average viewer. This means that the benchwork supporting the model railroad or the shelf supporting the diorama must be high enough so that the hills or structures along the rear of the scene are within six inches or so of the height of the viewer's eyes.

The Horizon

Chunk Spinks' HO scale modular layout is built in an inside corner, a portion of a model railroad that fits snugly inside the corner of a room (Figures 10-1 and 10-2). Near-

Fig. 10-1. Chuck Spinks' HO scale modular model railroad is a 4 x 4-foot inner corner with a curved HO West! backdrop.

115

Fig. 10-2. The city in Chuck Spinks' module is more realistic when viewed from near the track level rather than from overhead.

ly every item in his module, from the Woodland Scenics ground-foam grass to the buildings to the Walther's Instant Horizon backdrop is a commercial product. Chuck blended these elements together to create some very credible close-up details, like the cracked concrete street and the dirt alley to the right of the scene. He also did some careful color matching. The brickwork on the plastic kit structures was painted in about the same shades of red as the two-dimensional buildings that Tom Daniels painted on the master scene for the Walthers printing process. Chuck was also wise enough to know that the backdrop

should be curved around the corner to camouflage the actual joint between the two corner walls. The walls still have that joint, of course, but the Walthers backdrop, mounted on a curved piece of Masonite, hides the actual corner. He also aligned the backdrop so that it would appear to be a continuation of the modeled street when viewed from about 9 inches above the table (Figure 10-2). When viewed from about 2 feet above the table, which places the layout at about a conventional table height of 30 inches, the scene is far more toy-like. The lesson here is that the layout itself should be placed near eye level for

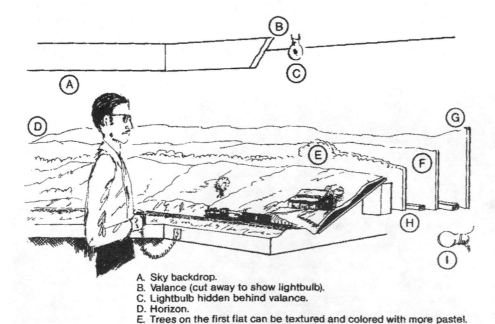

A. Sky backdrop.
B. Valance (cut away to show lightbulb).
C. Lightbulb hidden behind valance.
D. Horizon.
E. Trees on the first flat can be textured and colored with more pastel.
F. Middle flat can be covered with cutout art or photomurals.
G. Rear flat must be at eye level to convey the illusion of the horizon.
H. Background flats provide the three-dimensional effect of hills.
I. Lighting for the horizon is placed below the scenery and flats.

Fig. 10-3. A cutaway view of the optimum arrangement for a shelf-style model railroad. The three background flats are spaced only an inch or two apart. They are staggered here to show their shapes and the 1 x 1 supporting blocks.

maximum realism. One of the advantages of a model railroad, particularly one built on a shelf for an around-the-wall layout, is that it fills the viewer's peripheral vision on both sides. The effect is the same as a wide-angle movie screen is to a viewer seated in the front of the theater. You are drawn directly into the scene, so you automatically feel that you are part of that imaginary world.

Figure 10-3 portrays the ideal method of building and lighting a model railroad. First, the layout is placed high enough so that the mountains extend almost to eye level. Remember, the real horizon is at eye level. When you are relatively close to any mountains or hills, they mask the true horizon. The model scene must reproduce this effect by having the mountain peaks extend as high as you would *expect* them to.

The scene in Figure 10-3 is one of rolling foothills; the distant hills extend only to eye level to *imply* that you could see the valley *beyond*. If the scene depicted true mountains, the background flats or hills would have to be positioned at least a foot higher. In fact, if the tabletop or track level is at about chest level, the mountains would extend far enough above the horizon so that flats or painted mountains would be unnecessary; only a distant blue-sky backdrop need be installed. This is one reason why mountain scenes are so popular with modelers. With some thoughtful planning and construction, you can incorporate the lessons of Figure 10-3 and make rolling hills or farmland as realistic as mountains. The background flats would have to be placed only an inch or two apart to give a three-dimensional effect.

Blue-Sky Backdrops

Every model railroad should be constructed so that the walls of the room or any visible areas behind the layout are completely hidden with a sky backdrop that extends from the tabletop all the way to the ceiling. Some museum dioramas even curve the vertical blue-sky backdrop over to the roof of the room, but that's not worth the trouble on a model railroad; the viewer's eye should be directed at the scene, not at the ceiling. If your model railroad has a rear edge of 8 feet or less, consider using a single piece of 1/8-inch hardboard like Masonite. This material can be curved for inside corners (Figure 10-1) if it is supported every 6 inches or so with wooden blocks along the backs of the horizontal edges. For most model railroads, however, the backdrop must be much longer; even a 4 x 8-foot layout will usually have a backdrop with one curved corner connecting one 4-foot and one 8-foot edge to require at least an 11-foot-long backdrop. The best material for such backdrops is the least-expensive grade of linoleum or vinyl floor covering. If you can find 36-inch-wide hall runners, use them. If not, buy the 6-foot-wide material and split it into two 3-foot pieces. The only limit on the

length of this linoleum is the amount of weight you can lift a 25-foot roll is about maximum. The most likely sources for 36-inch linoleum are stores like Sears, Penneys, or Montgomery Ward. Aluminum flashing, for the peaks and valleys of roofs, is available in 24-inch widths and rolls up to 30 feet. The aluminum surface must be sanded before painting to avoid easily chipped paint.

Since the linoleum can be ordered in almost any length, you won't have to camouflage the seams with patches that will eventually crack; you would, however, have to patch the Masonite. Avoid flowery patterns of linoleum because the pattern may show through as shadows. The colors on Reference Card 24 allow you to blend true sky blue at the top of the backdrop with a lighter blue at the horizon by mixing in more white as you paint the backdrop from top to bottom. Apply the paint with a 4-inch-wide roller and paint the entire length with each color mix, blending the ever-lighter shades of blue down to the horizon (Figure 10-4).

Photomurals and Painted Backdrops

There is some disagreement, even among museum diorama builders, as to whether a photomural or a painted backdrop is more realistic. The problem with the photomural is that it is more realistic than the foreground. This can be overcome if you have the nerve to spray a light

Fig. 10-4. With a narrow roller, paint the deep blue of the upper sky to blend gradually into a white-blue near the horizon. Twist the roller for puffy clouds, and use just a trace of paint for horizontal wisps.

wash of gray-white over the expensive photomural with an airbrush, The wash lends the misty look of faraway scenes and softens the harsh colors in the mural. If you wish to make photomurals from your own color negatives, ask your local camera shops for prices. Expect to pay several hundred dollars for even a 4-foot photo in four colors. The best alternatives are the printed photomurals for model railroads from Vollmer (a city scene and a mountain/valley scene) and Faller (superb mountains, foothills, and farmland). Some wallpaper shops also carry photomurals for interior decorating. Some of these murals may have scenes that are the proper size and style for model railroads, but they are also in the hundred-dollar-and-up price range.

The most effective painted backdrops are those made by Walthers (Instant Horizons), Detail Associates, and JMC

Fig. 10-5. Bill Peters used textured flats for the weed-covered hills and cutout color photographs and calendar art for the backdrop of this S scale scene.

Fig. 10-6. Jack Rice's backdrop scene is a collage of Detail Associates and several Walthers backdrop scenes cut from the backdrop and cemented to a painted sky.

International. The Detail Associates backdrops and Walthers' Instant Horizons are designed to be used as profile cutouts; you cut out the outlines of the tops of the hills, mountains, or structures with scissors and glue them to the backdrop with rubber cement. It's more realistic if you actually use these profiles as flats by gluing them to stiff plastic For Sale signs, pieces of Masonite hardboard or 1/8-inch thick "Foam-Core," a polystyrene board with treated cardboard on both sides so the foam becomes the "core" of the board. The Foam-Core board is available at art supply stores. The plastic, Masonite or Foam-Core should first be cut to match the upper outline of the hill, mountain, or structure profile (see Figures 10-5 and 10-6). Cut them about 1/8 inch smaller so that the paper cutout protrudes that much above the plastic, Masonite or Foam-Core. This hides the thickness of it. (Do not use cardboard; it will warp from changes in humidity.) Color the white edges of the cutouts with felt-tipped pens to match the scenes.

The flats can be positioned just an inch or two in front of the sky-blue linoleum backdrop to provide a three-dimensional effect to the horizon (see Figure 10-3). This technique can be used effectively by cutting out individual hills and mountains from the Faller or Vollmer photomural backdrops. The profile or flats technique allows you to use a single scene several times by purchasing duplicates of the scene and overlapping the hills, mountains, or structures to vary the appearance, but not the colors. If you are cramped for space, glue the cutout profiles directly to the sky backdrop. It is also possible to combine photomurals with Walthers or Detail Associates backdrops, or even to cut out calendar photos to create a single scene (see Figure 10-6).

Forced Perspective

The basic artistic rule of perspective is that the sizes of objects appear to diminish in direct proportion to their distance from the viewer. Hence, objects nearer the horizon appear to be much smaller than when viewed close up. A perfectly straight road appears to form a point as it reaches toward the horizon. You can bend this rule to make your scenes seem much larger by using smaller scale objects near the back of the scene. For example, if you are modeling a small town that is built on rolling hills, use HO scale (1/87) houses for the foreground with N scale (1/160) houses midway between the foreground and the sky backdrop and Z scale (1/220) houses nearest the backdrop. The sizes of the trees on Hal Riegger's N scale layout (Figure 10-7) seem to be the same size all the way up the mountain; in fact, the trees near the crest are only about 1/2 inch high. Be sure to provide a hilltop to break any perspective that continues onto a painted or photomural backdrop (Figure 10-8). If the road is allowed to run over the crest of even a gentle hill, it can be repeated on the backdrop, but with the bottom of the road just a bit narrower to suggest that the road is farther away. This technique will also be effective where rivers or streams must appear on both the backdrop and on the diorama or model railroad.

Lighting the Scene

The correct way to display an oil painting is to illuminate it with a clamp-on light above it or with a ceiling-mounted spotlight. Either spotlighting method can be

Fig. 10-7 The spirea-weed trees on Hal Riegger's N scale layout were deliberately made smaller as they reached the top of the mountain to create a forced perspective. The mountain itself was made from broken chunks of insulating foam from a wrecked refrigerator car.

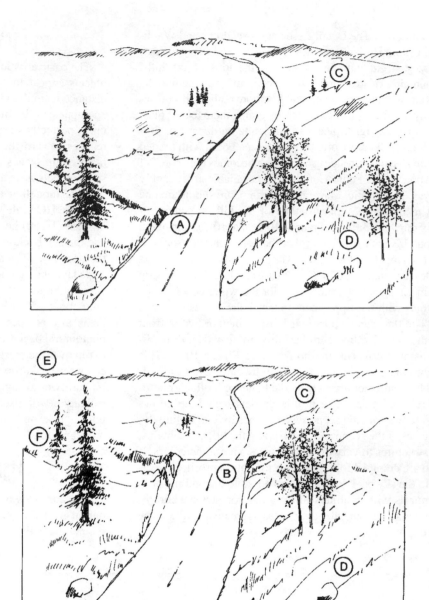

Fig. 10-8. The "incorrect" (top) and "correct" (bottom) methods of leading a three-dimensional road (or river) onto the painted image of the backdrop road.

A. End of modeled road should not abut painted or photographed road; impossible to disguise joint.
B. Modeled road disappears over crest of hill, then reappears in reduced width to suggest perspective.

C. Painted or photo backdrop.
D. Modeled scenery.
E. Painted horizon near eye level.
F. Top of scenery may be below eye level.

used to illuminate a small diorama that rests on a bookshelf. Lighting for a large model railroad, however, is a more complex task.

Sunlight or Bright Shade?

You have two choices of illumination for any model scene: fluorescent lighting, which produces an effect much like bright shade in the outdoors, or incandescent lighting, which produces sharp shadows similar to sunlight. Fluorescent lighting is more cost-efficient, but it can produce a negative psychological effect on the viewer. Just as cloudy days can be depressing, so can fluorescent lighting. If your model depicts an abandoned mine or a battle scene, fluorescent lighting may produce the precise effect you are searching for. Winter or late fall scenes (see Chapter 12) can also be more effective when viewed under fluorescent lighting.

The colors and shadows of a model scene illuminated by incandescent lighting have an added warmth that makes its slightly higher cost worth the trouble. Small 50-watt miniature floodlight bulbs are relatively inexpensive to burn compared to fluorescent lighting of equal intensity, and they produce an excellent shadow effect. Remember, shadows help to define river details, the grain in scale wood, and the textures of rocks, dirt, grass, weeds, and clutter. Textures are considerably more defined by the shadows of incandescent lighting. Thus, they appear more realistic to most viewers. Lighting shops sell a variety of inexpensive fixtures that can be hidden behind valances for mounting 50-watt floodlights. Some decorative swivel lamps and reflectors also will accept these bulbs. The lighting fixtures can then be matched to the decor of a formal den or study.

Backlighting the Horizon

The most important position for any lighting system for illuminating models is one where the light is directed from either over or from behind the viewer's head. This direct lighting is necessary to highlight the details on the models. What many model railroaders forget, however, is that the horizon usually appears to be brighter than the foreground. The rear edges and the backdrops of most model railroads are almost always darker than the foreground. Much of the realism of any scene is lost with this type of lighting. The ideal lighting positions for a model railroad are shown in Figure 10-11.

Few modelers have the foresight to leave just an inch or two open between the back of the scenery and the sur-

Fig. 10-10. The curve in the corner of this linoleum background is just visible, as are the 1 x 3 supports for the linoleum and the valance to the ceiling that hides the lights from the viewer.

Fig. 10-9. Ceiling-mounted spotlights and backdrop lights behind the valance illuminate this shelf-style railroad built by Bill Peters to exhibit PBL S-scale model railroad products.

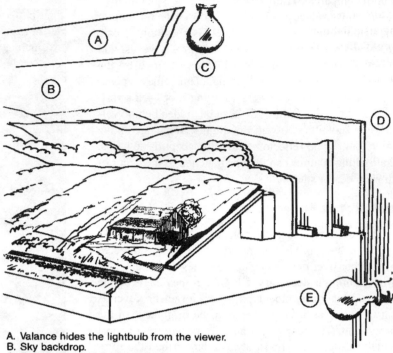

A. Valance hides the lightbulb from the viewer.
B. Sky backdrop.
C. For the effect of sunlight, the upper lights should be placed as close to the front of the benchwork as possible.
D. The horizon, new eye level.
E. To duplicate the brighter lighting effect of the sky and horizon, place the lightbulb below the layout.

Fig.10-11. A close-up view of Figure 10-3. The foreground (upper) lighting and the horizon lighting (lower right) exemplifies maximum "outdoor" lighting realism.

face of the backdrop. The gap can be filled with one or two rows of flats (see Chapter 9) and still leave plenty of space for the passage of light from below the table. If you lack even those couple of inches, the best place for the horizon lighting is in the corner, where the wall and the

backdrop meet the ceiling. Shield the bulbs in this area with a short valance that allows the lights to shine on the layout alone. Some modelers use this type of lighting with several ceiling-mounted spotlights shining from the access aisles above the operator's and spectators' heads

Fig. 10-12. Albert Hetzel's O scale shelf-style layout has a curved backdrop in this corner, with horizon lights hidden behind a valance and foreground lights overhead.

(Figure 10-12). A track-lighting system sold by lighting fixture stores would be ideal for this type of horizon lighting/aisle lighting combination. The track lighting system would allow you to move the lights for the foreground to minimize overlapping shadows or dark areas and to add or subtract lights as needed to achieve the proper effect.

Preventing or Creating Shadows

One of the major problems that a modeler faces with lighting that simulates direct sunlight is the presence of overlapping shadows from two different lights. Even the shadow from a single light is not crisp enough to match the effect of the sun. The simplest solution to the problem is to be certain that no buildings, people, telephone poles, or other vertical objects cast their shadow on a light-colored surface. You may have to repaint some light-colored concrete streets to simulate darker blacktop because the blacktop won't allow the shadows to show. Some extra dark brown weathering can be applied to any buildings or ground that are too light (see Chapter 11). A small metal valance can be cut from an aluminum pie pan and attached to the ceiling to shield just that portion of the light pattern that produces the double shadow in places where the shadow's cast is darker than the scene. One of the incidental effects of the weathering technique in Chapter 11 for buildings and figures is that the recesses of the model's texture are darkened and the faces are highlighted. These effects are precisely those produced by sunlight. These shadow and highlight effects can be carried even further on models that cannot possibly be displayed in the proper light. Use an airbrush and a wash of 19 parts Polly Scale dark brown or dark gray paint to 19 parts water. The shadow wash must be applied before the model is placed in the scene. Spray the wash from *below* the model's shape to produce a shadow effect on, for example, the bottom edges of windowsills and under the eaves of roofs, anywhere a dark shadow would appear in real life. You can carry this effect a step further and actually *paint* the darker shadow on the ground of the scene with the same wash. The technique can be especially useful when the diorama or model railroad must be illuminated with fluorescent lights.

Fig. 10-13. The camera captures the glow of indoor and outdoor scale-size lighting as white stars on Jock Oliphant's award-winning mine diorama.

Lighting in Miniature

Model railroad shops stock a variety of scale-model streetlights and assorted light bulbs that range in size from a flashlight bulb to the tiny bulb that's often called a "grain of rice." Most of these bulbs are about 18 volts. If you supply them with just 3 to 9 volts, you'll obtain a scale amount of glow and increase the life of the bulb nearly tenfold. Most model railroaders use this lighting for night scenes, but the glow from even 3 volts is still visible under most indoor lighting conditions. Jock Oliphant's mine diorama used lighting as one of many superdetails that helped earn the scene the best-display award at an annual NMRA model-building contest (Figure 10-13). The illumination on the inside of the buildings calls attention to the interior details by making those details visible even under simulated daylight conditions.

Lighting in miniature is one of those details that must be planned when the model is being constructed so that the wires can be hidden inside walls or hollow poles made from brass or aluminum tubing. The wires lead beneath the scenery to either a small transformer or a battery holder with some nicad batteries. Electronics hobby stores, such as Radio Shack or Allied Radio, can provide the proper transformer and battery holders if you show them the types of bulbs you will be using. Be sure to protect the bulbs from surrounding wood, plastic, or other flammable materials with small heat shields made from two layers of aluminum foil. The foil can also serve as a reflector for the light.

CHAPTER 11

The Art of Weathering

A typical example of a weather-beaten structure is an old barn, its paint so faded that the only visible color is the silvery gray of old wood. Weathering is a term coined by modelers to describe the techniques used to capture the appearance of that barn in miniature. Any man-made object that sits outdoors shows the effects of weather, so any truly realistic diorama or model railroad scene should also display some degree of weathering. Natural weathering is essentially a three-part process. Wind blows dirt onto the building, rain and dew hold that dirt in place or streak it, and the sun fades the surface. The effects of industry, like smoke stains on a chimney top or powdered concrete stains on a covered hopper car, also fall into the weathering category. The deliberate destruction from simulated bombings for military dioramas can be achieved with the same modeling techniques.

Basic Weather-Beating in Miniature

If you truly want to improve the realism of your miniatures, invest about $190 in a single-action, internal-mix airbrush, an air-pressure regulator, and an air compressor. The Walthers and JMC catalogs provide several choices, or you can find the equipment at your hobby shop or artists' supply shop. The airbrush is just a miniature version of the spray guns used to paint automobiles. It produces a spray pattern that can be adjusted from something as tiny as the periods on this page to a circle about 2 inches in diameter. The advantage of the airbrush is that it gives you complete control over where you apply the paint, plus the ability to mix colors and washes that are not possible with aerosol cans of paint. For large painted areas, the airbrush allows you to use relatively odor-free paints like Polly Scale or Model-Flex. For scenery modeling, it has the particular advantage of producing automatically the gentle shaded edges of color changes that occur so often in the real world. The gentle blend of black paint, to imitate soot stains on the chimney in Figure 11-1, could have been achieved only with an airbrush. Most weathering ef-

fects in the real world are the result of wind-borne soot or dirt, and the airbrush provides a perfect method of actually duplicating wind as well as the color of the dirt and soot. The airbrush is not the only method of achieving weathering effects; the dark vertical stains on the power house in Figure 11-1 were done by streaking the still-fresh weathering colors with a number 00 paint brush and water before they could dry completely.

Fig. 11-1. Dr. Logan Holtgrewe's HO scale power plant has been weathered with a subtle black shadow applied with an airbrush.

Real World Weathering

The moment you drive a new car out of the showroom, it begins to depreciate and it begins to be affected by the real world. Drive that car just a few blocks and the sun will begin to fade the paint, the wind will blow dust over it, you'll likely hit at least one water splash, and the tires will kick up more dirt and water. Leave that new car outdoors for a couple of weeks and it will look years older. You've subjected your shiny new car to the effects of weathering.

Unfortunately, most modelers paint their miniatures and house them in protected environments where the real world weather cannot reach them. If you want really realistic models, simulate the effects of nature.

Basically, there are only about six aspects of weathering that you'll want to simulate (to at least some degree) on a model: (1) the bleaching or whitening effect of the sun's ultraviolet rays, (2) the oxidizing effects of the sun to dull the finish, (3) the effect of the wind blowing sand to literally sand-blast the paint, (4) the effect of rain washing wind-blown and collected dirt onto and down the surfaces, (5) the effect of wear in the form of chips or, on handrails and steps, bare metal or rust showing through where feet or hands have rubbed, and (6) the effects of age or the item rotting, settling, sagging, or leaning.

Keep that list in mind when you study a photograph of a real world scene you wish to duplicate. The more of these weathering items that are visible, the older the building, car, or locomotive is likely to be.

For a model, you have to start with something that is not shiny because we are not illuminating our models with the sun. For maximum realism, a brand-new model car should have a semi-gloss finish — the weathering and fading takes over from that dull shine.

The Five-Step Weathering Technique

The formulas on Reference Card 25 provide shortcuts for achieving the appearance of natural weather effects on virtually any model. They are applied with a brush, so if you are using an airbrush, add more water or alcohol as suggested on Reference Card 7. For that final dusty effect (Step 4), use artist's pastel chalks; the oil-base pastel sticks will not powder effectively. The chalks can be reduced to powder by rubbing them on a piece of sandpaper and catching the dust in a small jar. The pastel chalk powder can then be brushed on wherever you would normally find weathering. Never rub the chalks directly onto the model: use them only as powders. To simulate particularly dirty surfaces, such as rain-washed concrete on a covered hopper car, wet the brush before you streak on the powdered pastel chalks. The chalks produce roughly four times the color intensity when applied to a wet surface or with a wet brush. For medium effects, apply a light overspray of Testors DullCote (Step 5) to seal the first pastel chalk application, then do a second application of chalk. The DullCote will fade the pastel colors and soften their effect, so you may have to repeat Steps 4 and 5 two or three times to retain the effect you want and still have the protection of the final clear coat of DullCote.

Weathering Brick and Stone Walls

The weathering technique on Reference Card 25 makes it easy to simulate the appearance of older brick or stone walls. Many stone, brick, and wooden walls and fences in the real world have painted-on signs. The signs can be applied with dry transfers, such as Clover House, Woodland Scenics, Vintage Reproductions' Ice in Figures 11-3, 11-4, and 11-5. Microscale makes sign decals that can be used directly on the brick, stone, or wood-textured walls or fences. The decals, however, must be covered with at least six applications of decal-softening fluid like Microscale Micro Sol so that the decal will snuggle in against the textured surface. With care, these techniques will work on paper or cardboard with printed-on brick, stone, or wood colors, but the techniques are far more effective when the texture is three-dimensional, as it is on molded-plastic or cast epoxy brick, stone, or wood walls.

Weathering Wood

Weathered wood can be made in miniature from bass or balsa wood or by scraping simulated wood grain into strips of plastic with a razor-saw blade. To simulate the silver-gray color of barnwood and older wooden trestles, use the Five-Step Weathering Technique. Match the color of the real wood or a photograph of the wood to one of the colors on Reference Card 8 and proceed with the weathering technique. You may want to add an additional color for older woods. The effect of moss on the north side of the wood can be simulated by spraying on a wash of the sage green weed and foliage color from Reference Card 17, mixing in a total of 19 parts water to 1 part Polly Scale avocado and applying the wash with an airbrush. On older weathered buildings, some of the planks will probably have broken under the weight of winter snows or hard winds (Figure 11-6). Plastic can be used for this type of wood, but it is easier to use real wood and break it into splinters. If you paint the wood with the same technique used to paint the plastic, you can mix wood and plastic as simulated wood in the same structure or fence.

Fig. 11-2. Before the weathering process: A typical HO scale structure, converted from kits.

Fig. 11-3. Vintage Reproductions dry transfers can be burnished onto the surface by rubbing the backing with a soft lead pencil.

Fig. 11-4. A wash of 19 parts water to 1 part Polly Scale black paint was applied to the structure to represent decades of rain-washed locomotive soot.

Weathering Rocks and Cliffs

The Five-Step Weathering Technique will allow you to add effective superdetails to rocks and cliffs. Use pre-colored plaster and water-soluble paint with the staining techniques in Chapter 4 for rocks and cliffs placed several feet away from the viewer. For close-up scenes and dioramas, though, paint rock castings to complement their textures and make them indistinguishable from real rocks using the Five-Step Weathering Technique. Look at your photographs of the area you are modeling to see if the real rocks and cliffs have moss growing on the north or well-shaded sides. About a quarter of all the rocks in any mountainous area have this effect. The sage green on Reference Card 17 is close to the color that is visible on most of the northern surfaces of rocks and cliffs in the Rocky Mountains and Sierras. Some additional gray or green can be added to simulate the colors of mosses in other areas,

Fig. 11-5. After the weathering process: The building shows decades of exposure to the elements.

Fig. 11-6. This HO scale creosote company on the Sverna Park Model Railroad club layout shows years of neglect with broken boards, torn signs and rain-washed soot and dirt.

including the brighter green mosses near streams and lakes. The moss color should be applied as a paint, not a wash, using an airbrush to control the paint flow and give the spattered effect of real moss.

Weathering Signs

Any signs that you apply should show the effects of cracking or fading from wind or sun. These effects should be completed before using the Five-Step Weathering Technique. You can rub off portions of the sign with 600-grit emery paper or fine steel wool to simulate the effects of wind and sun on the sign. Paper signs or advertisements on full-size structures can be duplicated with paper signs. Walthers and Chooch offer billboard signs from 1930 to 1990. Microscale offers decals and Clover House, Vintage Reproductions, and Woodland Scenics offer full-color sheets of scale-size signs reproduced from advertisements from the 1930s to the present. You can also find suitable signs in magazines or you can even use canceled postage stamps.

Fig. 11-7. Rock faces near the foreground can be weathered to simulate the rough texture of real rocks.

Fig. 11-8. The weathering technique can be used for military dioramas, but with black to duplicate fire and smoke stains, as Russell Mueller did with this 1/32 scale "bombed building" kit.

Paper signs should be treated with the following technique to reduce their thickness to something approximating scale-size paper. Place the cutout sign in a cup of water overnight. Remove the sign from the water and place it face down on a paper towel laid over a flat, hard surface. With your index finger, gently rub the back of the sign until little balls or threads of paper roll away. Continue rubbing until only the ink and a trace of paper remains. You may have to add more water during the process. Pick up the sign with tweezers and apply it to the wall or fence that has been coated with bonding agent (Reference Card 13). If necessary, dip your fingertip in water and press the paper sign firmly into the surface of the wall or fence. Allow the sign to dry for about three days, then weather it with 600-grit emery paper or fine steel wool. If fine hairs or fibers are still visible, spray the sign with a light coat of Testors' DullCote and let it dry for a day. The paper can then be sanded again lightly with 600-grit emery paper to smooth the surface. The sign can now be weathered with the Five-Step Weathering Technique.

Battle Damage for Dioramas

The bomb-damaged diorama in Figure 11-8 shows how realistic the Five-Step Weathering Technique can be. Russell Mueller used cast-plaster walls for the structures and balsa wood for the floors and loose beams. Several kit manufacturers mold the loose brick and crumbling mortar effect directly into the plaster material. Some firms also offer products to simulate the piles of rubble. Some of the inexpensive Airfix and the Lesney/Matchbox all-plastic diorama kits also have suitable battle-damaged walls for 1/87 through 1/76 scale dioramas. Individual bricks can be cut from balsa wood and added to the piles of rubble. Pile the rubble until you are satisfied with its shape, then form the piles into rigid units using soaking agent and bonding agent, as shown in Figures 6-2, 6-3, and 6-4.

CHAPTER 12

The Seasons and the Desert

One of the fundamental lessons of creating a credible model is to restrict that model to everyday scenes rather than dramatic ones. There is an extremely thin line between the unusual effects that nature produces and caricatures of nature. The beauty of an autumn scene, the stillness of a snow-covered station, or the drama of a desert are difficult to ignore as inspirations for any miniature scene. It certainly is possible to create a realistic diorama or model railroad with dramatic scenic effects like these, but it takes far more skill than modeling familiar scenes. The desert is included in this chapter because its character is as difficult to capture in miniature as an autumn or winter scene.

Autumn in Miniature

The brilliant rainbow of color that typifies autumn in the East and the golden yellow of aspens in the Rockies can be irresistible to modelers. The Buhl Science Center's autumn diorama, pictured in the color section, shows what can be accomplished with color. Dick Harley and Dave Hussey's aspen tree leaves are made with the paper punchings from check cancellations. The rainbow effect is easy to carry too far for a realistic scene; most of the colors you would expect to see are too bright to be realistic on a model. Buhl Science Center's master modeler Charles Bowdish uses gray-white in the color mix to subdue the colors slightly. This makes them more pastel than those in a photograph of an eastern autumn. AMSI and Noch offer ground foam in autumn colors and Woodland Scenics produces foliage material in fall shades, so you do not necessarily have to create your own colors. if you find these brands to be too bright, a light wash of light gray Polly Scale paint can be sprayed over the trees to give the slightly hazy effect that is the most realistic for miniatures.

Winter Scenes

The snow-covered scenes of winter are well worth attempting, particularly for a diorama. If you don't want a complete winter diorama, you could duplicate winter's lingering snows near the tops of mountain passes. In some respects, a snow scene is even easier to create than a summer scene. The basic scenery shapes must still be constructed with the Hydrocal and paper towel method, and any cliffs or other rock textures must be installed and painted. Roads should also be covered with dirt or simulated pavement. Other grass or dirt textures don't have to be installed, however, because the dirt and plants usually appear only on relatively gentle slopes, the same gentle slopes that would capture and hold snow. In place of the usual dirt, grass, and weed textures, you would substitute snow texture directly over the Hydrocal hills.

You may want to use molding plaster or plaster of paris to shape snowdrifts behind fences and on the roofs of cabins or other structures. Icicles can be made by stringing artist's gloss medium over a sheet of glass with a toothpick. Shape the icicles with several layers of the gloss medium and, when dry, shave the icicles from the glass with a razor blade. Attach them to the eaves of buildings and to rock cliffs to simulate frozen rivulets and springs with one of the thickened cyanoacrylate cements, such as Goldberg Super Jet or Hot Stuff Super T.

Fig. 12-1. Snowdrifts were shaped in plaster on the roof and ground, then baking soda was sifted over the scene. The dead tree is made from five weed roots with a trunk shaped from automobile body putty.

Snow for Modelers

Every white powder known to man has been used by modelers to simulate snow. You can try your favorite, but be warned that nearly everything except common baking soda has some drawbacks. (Never use baking powder, which dissolves into a mudlike mess.) To apply baking-soda snow, spray the area with the soaking agent to moisten it (Reference Card 12). Pour on enough bonding agent to cover the area. The bonding agent will prevent the snow from scattering into unwanted areas. The baking soda can then be sprinkled over the area with a tea strainer (Figure 12-2). Tap the sides of the tea strainer with your finger to help control the flow of the baking soda.

Study some photos of winter scenes to be sure you're getting the snow into the right shapes and the right places. The roofs of moving railroad cars, for instance, seldom have visible snow, but snow does accumulate on the pilots of locomotives. Standing freight cars accumulate as much snow as any nearby structures, of course. The places where snow falls are fairly obvious, but remember to avoid placing snow in the areas where it would usually

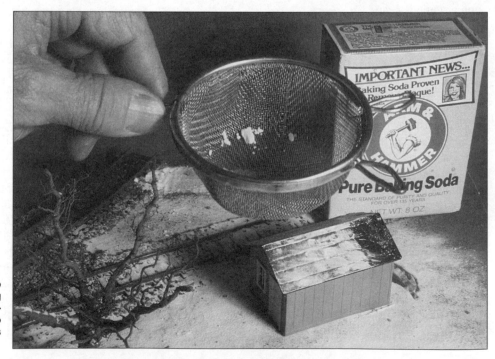

Fig. 12-2. Use a tea strainer to apply the baking soda, tapping the side of the strainer to control the flow of baking soda so it falls in the same patterns as real snow.

Fig. 12-3. Betty and Laddy Dick used baking soda "snow" in this HO scale scene. The soda was sprinkled onto the rails, then "plowed" with a stick.

melt away. You can scrape the snow from the tops of rail-road-track rails, but avoid getting it on any traveled portions of roads. To be safe, cut some newspaper masks to match the shape of the roads and hold them in place with map pins until you have completed the application of the snow. Simulate patches of ice and melted snow with dabs of artist's gloss medium.

The Desert

The desert in the United States is considered to be only the area around Phoenix, Ariz., where saguaro cacti grow (Figures 1-10 and 2-12). The cactus can be modeled with green pipe cleaners, but the ready-to-use Cactus from MLR Manufacturing, Keil-Line, and Plastruct are more realistic replicas of saguaro for 1/160 through 1/76 scales. More common to just about any desert scene are the relatively sparsely leafed mesquite and creosote bushes and clumps of yucca. These can be duplicated with fine-grind foam-textured lichen and macrame fiber as described in Chapter 7. Nearly all of these plants flower during the early spring, but the spring-like effect is difficult to capture

in miniature. Instead, recreate the desert the way it looks during the rest of the year.

The only portions of the desert that are flat are the bottoms of the dry lakes, and they, too, are difficult to simulate realistically. The seemingly flat portions of the desert are rolling hills and valleys with bare rock hills or mountains visible in the distance. Use rock castings extensively to capture this desert feeling. Of course, real sand dominates any desert scene. Apply it the same way as dirt is used as a color and texture in Chapter 6.

Above all, the feeling of isolation must be captured, as Wally Suggs has with his N scale modular scene (Figure 12-4). The simulated road can be scraped into the sand with the edge of a coarse-textured ink eraser or a Bright Boy track-cleaning eraser. Wally built the Indian hogan from broken tree twigs and plaster of paris. He used several shades of beige and mixed traces of Boxcar Red, gray, yellow, and brown for the various sand tones. These color variations were mixed as washes or with 1 part Polly Scale paint to 19 parts water to be sure the color changes were as subtle as possible. For illustrations of other desert scenes, see Figures 1-10 and 2-12.

Fig. 12-4. Wally Suggs captured the isolation of the desert by positioning shrubs sparsely and by applying alternate shades of beige paint with an airbrush to simulate different sand colors.

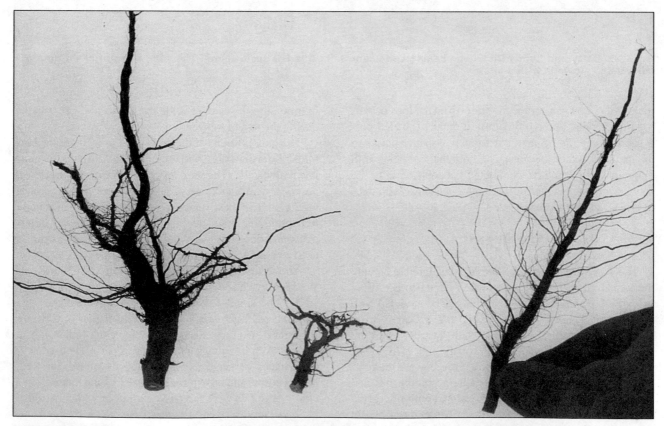

Fig. 12-5. The dried roots of larger weeds, particularly the bushy "tumbleweed" variety, make realistic bare tree forms for use in winter scenes, as well as for dead and partially dead trees in other seasons. Pull the weeds in late summer after a heavy rain so most of the tiny "hairs" remain, then trim and allow the root to dry for a month or more.

Sources of Supply

The best source for any scenery material is your nearest hobby dealer. For the names and addresses of the shops nearest you, look in the telephone book's Yellow Pages under the heading "Hobby and Model Construction Supplies, Retail." If your local shop does not have exactly what you need, ask a salesperson to order it from the manufacturer. If you want to obtain catalogs or other information from the manufacturer, always enclose a stamped, self-addressed envelope to ensure a reply. Most manufacturers charge for their catalogs, so ask for a current price. Some catalogs are only 25 cents, but others are as high as $10.

A.I.M. Products
P.O. Box 290092
Saint Louis, MO 63129
   Tunnel portals and retaining walls.

AMSI Scale Model Supplies
P.O. Box 750638
Petaluma, CA 94975
   Ground foam, Poly Fiber, texturing materials, trees, and roads.

Activa Products
P.O. Box 472
Westford, MA 01886
   Celluclay papier-mâché, Rigid Wrap plaster impregnated gauze, and Insta-Mold RTV rubber mold compounds.

American Art Clay Co., Inc.
4717 West 16th Street
Indianapolis, IN 46222
   Instant papier mâché, Sculpta-Mold, and Mix-A Mold RTV mold-making compounds.

Avalon Concepts
1055 Leisz's Bridge Road
Leesport, PA 19533
   Detail Wand and Power Station hot-wire cutters for polyurethane foam boards.

Bachmann Industries, Inc.
1400 East Erie Avenue
Philadelphia, PA 19124
   Ready-made trees and Styrofoam mountains,

Badger Air-Brush Co.
9128 Belmont Avenue
Franklin Park, IL 60131
   Badger airbrushes and Model-Flex paints.

Campbell Scale Models
P.O. Box 5307
Durango, CO 81301-6815
   Tree kits.

Celluclay (see Activa Products)

Chemco ETI
P.O. Box 365
Fields Landing, CA 95537
   Envirotex Lite and Chemco Ultra Glo casting resins.

Chooch Enterprises
P.O. Box 217
Redmond, WA 98073
   Cast resin junk piles, tunnel portals, and retaining walls.

Clover House
Box 62
Sebastapol, CA 95473-0062
   Dry-transfer signs and lettering.

Color-Rite Scenery Products
2041 Winnetka North
Minneapolis, MN 55247
   Tree kits and rock molds.

Detail Associates
P.O. Box 5357
San Luis Obispo, CA 93403
   Printed full-color backdrops.

E-R Model Importers, Ltd.
1000 S. Main St.
Newark, NY 14513
   Importers of Noch scenery products, Preiser figures, Busch and Praline vehicles.

Envirotex (see Chemco)
   Casting, resin for water.

Faller (see Wm. K. Walthers)
Trees, lichen, ground foam, roads, backdrops, and texturing materials.

Floquil-Polly S Color Corp. (see Testor Corp.)

Form-A-Mountain Co.
P.O. Box 29070
Providence, RI 02909
Surface-texturing material.

Granite Line (see Rock Quarry)
Ballast and scale-size rocks.

Heljan (see JMC International)
Building kits.

Highball Products (see Wm. K. Walthers)
Ballast and fine rocks.

Hydrocal (see U.S. Gypsum)

I.S.L.E. Laboratories
Sylvania, OH 43560
Mountains-in-Minutes RTV rock molds, pre-cast
foam rocks and retaining walls, trees, and casting compounds.

JMC International
1025 Industrial Drive
Bensenville, IL 60106
Lichen moss and LaBelle figures.

John's Lab
4915 Dean Street
Woodstock, IL 60098
Ballast and fine rocks.

K & S Scenery Products
P.O. Box 117824
Carrollton, TX 75011-7824
Individual leaves as "Broadleaf Foliage" and other scenery products.

Keil-Line, Inc.
6440 McCullom
Lake Road Wonder Lake, IL 60097
Cast metal cactus and detail parts.

Kibri (see Wm. K. Walthers or JMC International)
Trees, ground foam, flocking, texturing materials, roads, and backdrops.

LaBelle (see JMC International)
Plastic figures and modeler's oil and grease.

Life-Like Products, Inc.
1600 Union Avenue
Baltimore, MD 21211
Trees, lichen, texturing materials, and Styrofoam mountains.

Merten (see JMC International or Wm. K. Walthers)
Scale model figures.

Micro Scale Industries, Inc.
P.O. Box 11950
Costa Mesa, CA 92627
Decals for signs and highways.

Mini-Metal (see Original Whistle Stop)

Model-Flex (see Badger)

Model Power
180 Smith Street
Farmingdale, NY 11735
Trees, lichen, and figures.

Mountains-in-Minutes (see I.S.L.E. Laboratories)

Mr. Plaster
P.O. Box 23066
Toledo, OH 43623
Cast plaster retaining walls, pilings, junk, and tunnel portals.

N.J. International
77 West Nicholai Street
Hicksville, NY 11801
Lichen, trees, scale model people, and detail parts.

Noch (see JMC International or Wm. K. Walthers)
Trees, ground foam texturing materials, and roads.

Original Whistle Stop, Inc.
2490 East Colorado Boulevard
Pasadena, CA 91107
Mini-Metal cast-metal figures.

Pauls Model Railroad Shops
121 Lincolnway West
New Oxford, PA 17350
Sommerfeldt and other brands of imported products.

Pikestuff (see Rix)

Plastruct, Inc.
1020 South Wallace Place
City of Industry, CA 91748
   Trees, Poly Fiber, cactus, ground foam, and streets.

Polly Scale (see Testor Corp.)

Polyterrain, Inc.
2105 W. 18th St.
Fayetteville, AR 72701
   Texturing paste, glue, and casting resin for Styrofoam scenery.

Preiser (see Wm. K. Walthers or JMC International)
   Scale model figures.

RR&F (see Wm. K. Walthers)
   Textured highway materials.

Rix Products
3747 Hogue Road
Evansville, IN 47712
   Pikestuff and Rix highway details, bridges and structures.

Scale Link, Ltd.
R/O The Talbot Hotel
Blandford Road
Iwerne Minster, Dorset, DT11 8QN
England
   Etched brass leaves.

Scenic Craft, Inc.
Box 862
Edmond, OK 73034
   Molded-plastic pine trees.

Scenic Express
1001 Lowry Ave.
Jeannette, PA 15644-2671
   "Super Trees," ground foam, Noch and other scenery products.

Sherwin Williams Paints (see the telephone book's Yellow Pages under "Paint, Retail")

Smith & Sons
13630 G.A.R. Highway
Chardon, OH 44024
   Ballast and scale size rocks.

Sommerfeldt (see Pauls Model Railroad Shop)
   Flocking and flocked grass mats.

Sun Ray (see Walthers)
   Lichen, ground foam, ballast and other scenery products.

Testor Corporation
620 Buckbee Street
Rockford, IL 61104
   Testors, Floquil, Polly Scale and Polly S paints

Timber Products
2029 East Howe Avenue
Tempe, AZ 85281
   Ground foam flocking, weeds, texturing, and roads.

Ultra-Glo (see Chemco)

U.S. Gypsum Corporation (for the name of the nearest Hydrocal dealer, call 800-621-9626)

Vintage Reproductions
2606 Flintridge Drive
Colorado Springs, CO 80918
   Flocking, fake snow, and texturing materials.

Vollmer (see JMC International or Wm. K. Walthers)
   Ground foam, flocking, trees, backdrops, and texturing materials

Wm. K. Walthers, Inc.
5601 West Florist Avenue
Milwaukee, WI 53218
   Distributes a variety of different brands of scenery products to dealers and produces the Instant Horizons and Instant Buildings backdrops.

Woodland Scenics
P.O. Box 98
Linn Creek, MO 65052
   Ground foam, Poly Fiber, trees and tree kits, lichen, Lightweight Hydrocal plaster, rock molds, texturing paste, and dry-transfer signs.

Yankee Junction
P.O. Box 987
Lady Lake, FL 32659
   Printed full-color backdrops of sky and clouds.

Index

Reference Card 1
Nine-Step Scenery the Simple Way
(For more information refer to Chapter 1)

Step	Procedure	Chapter
1.	Locate photographs and color samples of real-life scenes	1 and 2.
2.	Build basic shape in Celluclay or plaster	1, 2, 3, and 4
3.	Add any rock castings or cliffs	2, 4, and 5
4.	Color surfaces with water-base paints	1 and 4
5.	Apply sifted dirt, ground foam, or other texture	3, 4, 6, 9, and 12
6.	Install trees and bushes	7
7.	Install ponds, streams, rivers, and other water effects	8
8.	Install structures, people, and other man-made features	1, 3, and 9
9.	Apply weathering with water-base paints	1, 4, 9, and ll

Reference Card 2
The Basic Do's and Don'ts for Realistic Scenery
(For more information refer to Chapter 1)

1. **DO** arrange lighting so that the background receives slightly more light than the foreground.
   DON'T build or color scenery under any lighting other than that used on the layout or diorama.

2. **DO** precolor all plaster or Hydrocal so that no white shows.
   DON'T try to paint every nook and cranny in the plaster.

3. **DO** apply a color wash to match the predominant earth color on all buildings and ground cover.
   DON'T place contrasting earth colors (such as red and beige) next to each other.

4. **DO** spray on a wash of light olive green to trees and shrubs to blend their colors.
   DON'T use out-of-the-box lichen moss or other texture that is kelly green without treating and coloring it.

5. **DO** use coal, petrified wood, and real rocks as patterns for latex rubber molds.
   DON'T use real rocks as-is for scenery.

6. **DO** use 1:1 epoxies or artist's gloss medium to simulate water.
   DON'T use casting resin and catalyst to simulate water.

7. **DO** use rock castings or retaining walls for slopes steeper than 45 degrees.
   DON'T apply grass or weeds to slopes steeper than 45 degrees.

8. **DO** include some gentle dirt- and weed-covered slopes beside tracks.
   DON'T use only rock cliffs or retaining walls on slopes beside tracks.

9. **DO** measure and record everything used in mixing plaster, colors, and resins so that you can duplicate them.
   DON'T attempt to match a color just by dabbing on a similar color.

10. **DO** refer to color pictures in magazines as prototypes for all scenery shapes and colors.
    DON'T try to duplicate someone else's scenery.

11. **DO** install a wraparound sky blue background (shaded to gray-blue at the horizon).
    DON'T paint anything other than sky and clouds on a backdrop.

12. **DO** build mountains or background city buildings at eye level.
    DON'T place any backdrop where the horizon is below eye level.

13. **DO** use several shades and sizes of ground foam, real dirt, and flocking for all loose textures.
    DON'T use untreated lichen, colored sawdust, or real pebbles for scenery.

14. **DO** use the exact natural shades shown in the color charts for all colors.
    DON'T use solid colors such as black, white, green, yellow, or brown for any scenery effects.

Reference Card 3
Paved Road Colors
(For more information refer to Chapter 3)

Material to be Simulated	Polly Scale Paint	Sherwin Williams Interior Latex Paint
Blacktop (Tar or Macadam)		
Undercoat gray	GrimyBlack414137	Heavy metal
Fresh tar wash	Reefer Gray 414116	Silhouette
Weathered tar wash	Tac Light Gray 505394	River Pebble
Fresh gravel wash	Dust 414305	1 part Origami White
		1 part Heavy Metal

Note: The wash mixture should be between 9 and 19 parts water to 1 part paint.

Concrete		
Weathered concrete	Dust 414305	1 part Origami White 1 Part Heavy Metal
Typical concrete	Concrete P414317	Metal Slippery Rock
Fresh concrete	Tac Light Gray 5050394	River Pebble

Note: At least two concrete colors should be blended in each section of concrete. Scrub on the darker color with a fine-pore sponge as a wash or 9 parts water to 1 part color.

Reference Card 4
Tools and Equipment, Materials and Containers for Simple Scenery
(For more information refer to Chapter 4)

Basic Tools and Equipment

Clothespins

Scissors

Staple gun

Spatula or palette knife

Ice-cream sticks and tongue depressors

Measuring spoon

Pyrex measuring cup

Steel ruler

Plastic basting syringe

Glass eye droppers

Awl or ice pick

Serrated kitchen knife

Sherwin Williams Decorator interior latex

Pin Vise

Magnet

Tweezers

Pump-style spray bottle for misting plants

Inexpensive paint brushes, sizes 0, 00, 0000, 2, 1/4", and 1/2"

Steel-bristle brush

Fine-pore sponge

Coarse-pore sponge

Rubber kitchen spatula

Floquil-Polly S standard color chart

Floquil-Polly S Model Railroad color chart

Butter knife

Flour sieve with screen-door-size screen

Tea strainer

Noch-brand electrostatic applicator for flocking

Emery paper, 600 grit

Single-edge razor blades

X-Acto or Zona razor saw

Masking tape

Airbrush, air pressure regulator, and air compressor (optional)

Basic Materials

Floquil-Polly S Paints

Sherwin Williams Decorator interior latex paints, or equivalent brand

Celluclay or papier-mâché

Hydrocal, molding plaster, and plaster of paris

Ground polyurethane foam

Artist's matte medium

Artist's gloss medium

Aluminum foil

Newspapers

Industrial-grade paper towels (brown or white)

Cotton gauze

Alcohol, denatured or isopropryl

Liquid dishwashing detergent

Macramé polypropylene twine

Pearl-white fingernail polish

Mason cement

Fabric dyes

Woodland Scenics foilage material

Electrical wire, 10 gauge

Plastic clothesline

Plastic wrap (like Saran Wrap)

Ultra-Glo or Envirotex epoxy resin

Basic Containers

Pyrex glass mixing tray for plaster

Flexible plastic mixing bowls for texture materials

5-gallon plastic buckets with snap-on lids (one for water, one for plaster of paris or Molding plaster, and one for Hydrocal plaster)

Plastic or glass jars and coffee cans with lids for storing textures, powdered colors, leftover precolored plaster, liquid dyes, washes, and specially mixed colors

Baggies or Ziploc plastic bags for storing textures

Reference Card 5
Liquid and Level Bulk Measures

1 teaspoon (1 tsp.) = 1.33 fluid drams

1 tablespoon (1 tbsp.) = 3 teaspoons

2 tablespoons (2 tbsp.) = 1 fluid ounce

4 fluid ounces = 1/2 cup

8 fluid ounces = 1 cup

16 fluid ounces = 1 pint

32 fluid ounces = 1 quart

128 fluid ounces = 1 gallon

Reference Card 6
Mixing Molding Plaster, Plaster of Paris, or Hydrocal
(For more information refer to Chapter 4)

1. Measure and mix thoroughly:
    2 cups cold water
    1 tablespoon dry powdered mason's cement or Rit liquid clothing dye

2. Mix thoroughly:
    1 measure of retarder as indicated on container or 1 tablespoon vinegar

3. Mix thoroughly:
    approximately 2 cups molding plaster or plaster of paris

4. Stir thoroughly while pouring powdered plaster into water until mixture reaches the consistency of whipping cream.

Note: Use Pyrex-type glass mixing containers and flexible cooking spatulas for mixing ingredients.

Reference Card 7
Polly Scale Paint Mixes for Airbrush Spray Painting
(For more information refer to Chapter 4)

Thinning Ratio with Water

4 parts Polly Scale paints 1 part water

4 drops liquid dishwashing detergent per pint of fluid
    Use about 25 pounds per square inch of air pressure.*

Note: For a wash, add 9 parts water (and detergent) to the paint/water mixture.

Thinning Ratio with Denatured Alcohol

3 parts Polly Scale paints

1 part denatured alcohol
    Use about 15 pounds per square inch of air pressure.*

Caution: Alcohol is extremely toxic. Spray it only in a well-ventilated area and wear a mask. Do *not* use isopropyl alcohol, which may contain glycerine or other additives that can retard the setting of the paint.

Thinning Ratio with Polly Scale Airbrush Thinner

3 parts Polly Scale paints

2 parts Polly Scale Airbrush Thinner
    Use about 1 5 pounds per square inch of air pressure.*

*Some airbrushes demand slightly more or less pressure, so experiment before painting the final model.
Clean the airbrush immediately after use. Acrylic paints, like Polly Scale, dry rapidly and can clog the airbrush.

Reference Card 8
Earth, Soil, and Rock Colors

(For more information, refer to Chapter 4)

Color	Applications	Artist's Acrylics	Polly Scale Paint	Sherwin Williams Interior Latex Paint
Black	Shadows or dulling washes only, not as color or wash itself	3 parts Lamp Black 1 part White	Grimy Black 414137	Black Hills
White	Not recommended	—	—	—
Off-white (chalk)	Chalk cliffs, mineral-salt deposits on edges of dried ponds	19 parts White 1 part burnt Sienna	Dirty White 505205	Antique White
Light gray	Limestone, some sandstone, cement or concrete	9 parts White 1 part Burnt Sienna	Dust 414305	1 part Origami White 1 part Heavy Metal
Medium gray	Limestone, granite, sandstone, cement or concrete	4 parts White 1 part Burnt Sienna	Tac Light Gray 505394	Silver Plate
Gray	Granite, basalt, sandstone, fresh or new concrete, blacktop roads	3 parts White 1 part Burnt Sienna	Reefer Gray 414116	Silouette
Beige or tan (light yellow)	Sandstone, some river sand	3 parts White 1 part Yellow Ochre	Mud 414314	Luminary Gold
Beige or Tan (medium yellow)	Sandstone, some river sand	1 part White 1 part Yellow Ochre	Earth 414311	Kinetic Khaki
Beige or tan (dark yellow)	Sandstone, some river sand, shale	9 parts Yellow Ochre 1 part Burnt Sienna	Sand Yellow 5050320	Cellini Gold
Beige or tan (Brown)	Sandstone, river sand, shale	9 parts Yellow Ochre 1 part Burnt Umber	Dirt 414308	Safari Brown
Beige or tan (Gray)	Sandstone, river sand, shale	9 parts Yellow 1 part black	OchreEarth 414311	Dromedary Camel
Pink or rose	Sandstone, basalt, granite, sand	8 parts White 1 part Indian Red 1 part Raw Sienna	2 parts Rust 4143323 1 part Caboose Red 414128 1 part Dirty White5050205	Courtley Rose
Clay or brick red	Clays, sandstone, sand	4 parts White 1 part Raw Umber	1 part Boxcar Red 414281 1 part CabooseRed 414128	Artful Auburn
Reddish brown (Light)	Sandstone, shale	1 part Burnt Sienna	Rust 414323 1 part White	Copper Bangle
Reddish brown (Medium)	Sandstone, shale	Burnt Sienna	Boxcar Red 414281	Carob Brown
Rich brown	Sandstone, shale, and farm soil	1 part Burnt Sienna 1 part Burnt Umber	Dirt 414308	Tortoise
Dark brown	Mudholes, river deltas, plowed earth	Van Dyke	Roof Brown 444414275	1 part Tortoise 1 part Heavy Metal

Note: Artist's Acrylics: Match colors to Polly Scale color chips by mixing as indicated.
Sherwin Williams interior latex paint: the names are from the Decorator series. These colors closely match Polly Scale paints and actual soil and rock colors.

Reference Card 9
The Foam Insulation Board and Felt Lightweight Scenery System
(For more refer to Chapters 5 and 6 and the Color Section)

Step 1: Build a lightweight plywood box to protect the vertical edges of one to four ayers of two-inch thick foam insulation board. If necessary, provide braces so the plywood, not the foam insulation board, supports the legs.

Step 2: Stack one to four layers of two-inch thick extruded-polystyrene foam insulation board. Dow-Corning's Styrofoam insulation board is blue, other brands are other colors. The white expanded-polystyrene bead board is not strong enough for a complete tabletop layout. Make the stack of two-inch thick boards thick enough to accommodate any valleys or canyons that will extend below the level of any roads, tracks or building sites. If there will be no valleys, a single layer of two-inch thick extruded-polystyrene foam insulation board is sufficient.

Step 3: Install all railroad tracks and ballast and roads or highways. Mark the locations of buildings and surrounding parking lots or any other horizontal flat surfaces.

Step 4: Use a hacksaw blade or a special hot-wire, drainage-ditch-cutting blade for Avalon Concepts DetailWand to cut drainage ditches or borrow pits on both sides of all railroad tracks and roads or highways. Use the bottom of these drainage ditches as the place to begin any upward slopes for cuts or cliffs and to begin the slopes of any embankments that will fall below the level of the tracks or roads.

Step 5: For hills or mountains that will rise above the extruded-polystyrene tabletop, use a hacksaw blade or hot-wire cutter to cut additional layers of the two-inch thick material to match the contours of the hills and mountains and stack these on the tabletop. Pin the contour-shaped foam boards together with three-inch-long concrete nails until you are satisfied with the final shapes, then cement the layers together with Woodland Scenics' Foam-Tack, Polyterrain's Paste or Liquid Nails' For Projects And Foamboard.

Step 6: For valleys, use a hacksaw blade or Avalon Concepts DetailWand hot-wire cutter to cut into the stack of polystyrene foam board at the desired angle for the valley's slopes. Remove any material from beneath the track and roadbed or highways where bridges will span valleys.

Step 7: Install any rocks , stone surface details, cliffs or retaining walls using Mountains-in-Minutes lightweight cast-urethane rocks and walls. Alternatively, model your own rock, stone or concrete faces using latex rubber molds and thin layers of still-wet plaster applied directly to the surface of the polystyrene surfaces. If you are modeling larger rivers or lakes, especially with rock shores or bottoms, install those at this time.

Step 8: Cover all the surfaces that are not horizontal building sites, parking lots, or highways with beige felt. Coat the surfaces to be covered with the felt with a very thick layer of latex contact cement and press the beige felt into the still-wet cement. When the contact cement dries, trim the felt away from the edges of the roads, the building sites and the railroad roadbed with a heavy-duty craft knife.

Step 9: Use a wire-bristle brush for cleaning machinists' files to tease the strands of the felt away from the surface.

Step 10: Select a latex paint in a shade of green to match photographs of real grass. Mix the paint with an equal part water and add a drop of detergent. Use an air brush or a pump-type sprayer to paint the felt. Apply just enough paint to color the teased strands so about 2/3 to 3/4 of the beige color is still visible. Allow at least 48 hours for the paint to dry.

Step 11: Sift real dirt through a fine-mesh tea strainer directly onto the felt. Use the wire brush to work the dirt into the fibers of the felt. When enough dirt is in place, those teased fibers will literally "grow" from the dirt, which is why I call this the Grass-That-Grows technique. Use fingernail scissors to trim the strands of the teased felt that stand more than 1/8 to 1/4 inch above the dirt. To create dirt roads, use scissors to trim the felt, then bury the felt completely with the sifted-on dirt.

Step 12: Sprinkle on some of the large granules of dirt to represent small rocks. Use small pebbles to create stream beds. Smaller streams can be modeled on top of the felt using pebbles for the streambed and artist's gloss medium for the water.

Step 13: Add some fine-grind foam in various shades of green to represent bushy-type weeds and bushes. Add some flocking or fiber strands to represent additional varieties of blade-type weeds.

Step 14: Mix 5 parts water to 1 part artist's matte medium and use a pump-type spray applicator to flood the felt with the mixture to bind all of the texturing together. You may need to use an eye dropper to flood really thick areas of sifted-on dirt for the dirt roads.

Reference Card 10
Dirt, Weed, Leaf, and Ground-Cover Textures

(For more information refer to Chapter 6)

Texture	Scenery	Sources of Texture
Dirt	Dirt	Pretest real dirt with a magnet. Do not use if magnetic. Sift through door screen, then through a tea strainer to produce medium and fine particles. (See Reference Card 11.)
Sand	Sand	Pretest real sand and sift as above.
Ground, foam Dirt	Dirt, sand, weeds, grass, leaves, pine needles	AMSI, Faller, Sun Ray, Timber Products, N.J., and Woodland Scenics
Sawdust	Not recommended	Sawdust is suitable only around a scale-model sawmill. For all other applications, us ground foam.
Flocking	Weeds, large pine needles	Precut flocking is available loose for use with an electrostatic dispenser and as preglued sheets. The best colors are made by Noch, Kibri, Timber Products. Vintage Reproductions, and Sommerfeldt, or cut flocking strands from macrame polypropylene twine.
Cattails	Weeds	The material inside tall cattails is the perfect size, color, and texture for weeds.
Foxtails	Weeds	The individual bristles of fall foxtails make perfect scale grass weeds. Some types have an inner core that simulates leafy weeds after the outer bristles are removed.
Paper punchings	Leaves	K & S Scenery Products and Noch have pre-colored leaf flakes as do some banks and Telex machines. The tiny holes made by somesmaller banks to cancel checks are often collected in thebase of the canceling machine.
Small stones, rubble, talus	Small stones, rubble, talus at the base of Cliffs	Left-over pre-colored molding plaster, plaster of paris, or Hydrocal. Place the leftovers in a cloth bag and pulverize with a hammer. Small batches of broken plaster can be lightly tinted by soaking them in a 50-50 mix of water and latex paint in the color used to highlight rock cliffs and moutainsides.

Reference Card 11
Testing Real Dirt for Modeling Suitability

(For more information refer to Chapter 6)

Test 1: Touch dirt with magnet to be certain soil is not magnetic. Discard the dirt if it is.

Test 2: Will dirt sift through a screen-door screen?

Test 3: Will the sifted dirt also sift through a tea strainer (half the gauge of screen-door screen)?

Test 4: Mix dirt with water and spread on metal pan to dry. If it cracks as it dries, it is clay and not suitable for scenery.

If all four tests are positive, sift dirt through door screen and store in coffee cans with snap-on lids. Match dirt color to Polly Scale color chip and label can with source of soil, color, and date.

Note: Dirt will be more pastel than any Polly Scale color. Mix Polly Scale dirt colors with 4:1, 9:1, and 19:1 pastel mixes of white and color to provide better color samples than too-dark, out-of-the-can colors for in-field soil selection.

Reference Card 12
Soaking Agent for Ground Cover, Dirt, and Ballast

(For more information refer to Chapter 6)

Isopropyl Alcohol (Rubbing alcohol from any drugstore)

Seal the base beneath the material with latex wall paint and allow the paint to dry completely.
Flood the area with alcohol.

Note: Alcohol helps to pull the bonding agent into the loose particles of dirt, ballast, or ground foam. It can be applied with an eye dropper or with a spray bottle in a well-ventilated area. Test the alcohol on plastic material by soaking a scrap for at least a week to be certain the alcohol does not melt or weaken the plastic.

Water-Soluble/Low-Odor Alternative

4 drops liquid dishwashing detergent
1 pint warm water

Mix thoroughly and apply with eye dropper or spray bottle until puddles of water are visible
between grains of ballast, dirt, or ground foam.

Apply bonding agent (Reference Card 13).

Reference Card 13
Bonding Agent for Loose Textures

(For more information refer to Chapter 6)

1 part artist's matte medium
3 parts water
4 drops liquid dishwashing detergent per pint of bonding agent

Mix thoroughly and apply with an eye dropper or spray bottle after applying the soaking agent (Reference Card 12).

Note: Common white glue can be used, but it is more likely to crack as it dries, and it is difficult to remove. Artist's matte medium dries with a flat finish and is more flexible, so the bonded material can be broken away from the base with a spatula if you must later alter the scene. Matte medium thickens in its container with age. Dilute it with as much as 8 parts water to 1 part matte medium.

Reference Card 14
Solvents and Thinners

Solvent	Disadvantages	Advantages
Water	Will not penetrate smaller gaps between granules of dirt, ballast, and ground foam. More suitable if a wetting agent is added (or about 4 drops liquid dishwashing detergent per pint of water). Can warp cardboard or wood if they are not thoroughly sealed with latex or other water-proof paint.	Easy clean up, no odor, nonflammable, inexpensive, and causes little staining or discoloration.
Isopropyl Alcohol (rubbing alcohol)	Extremely flammable (the flame is nearly colorless), toxic, and relatively expensive. Can stain or discolor surrounding ground foam or other colors. Can warp, bleach, and weaken some plastics. Most varieties not suitable as a paint thinner for Polly Scale or acrylics because they contain glycerin or other oils that prevent proper paint setting.	Soaks into and around just about any size dirt, ballast, or ground-foam granule. Will help pull or leach a water and matte medium solution into the bottom layers of dirt, ballast, or ground foam for better adhesion. Used as a thinner for Polly Scale and acrylic paints, it allows paint to flow better.
Denatured alcohol	Flammable, toxic, and expensive. Can stain or warp plastics and colors even more severely than isopropyl alcohol.	Same as isopropyl alcohol. Lack of glycerin or other oils makes it a better thinner than water and detergent. Allows Polly Scale and acrylic paints to flow better for more even coverage when applied with an airbrush.

Reference Card 15
Warning: The Dangers of Working with Alcohol

Denatured alcohol:

Can be used instead of water and detergent solution as a thinner for Polly Scale and acrylic paints. However, it is extremely toxic and flammable.

Isopropyl alcohol:

With a mixture of water, detergent, and artist's matte medium, it can be used as a setting agent for bonding dirt, ballast, or ground foam. The small amount of glycerin and oils contained in the alcohol are absorbed by the texturing material and don't seem to hinder the bonding of the matte medium. Do not use isopropyl alcohol as a paint thinner. The glycerin and oils prevent proper setting of the paint.

Caution: Never use either type of alcohol unless you are working in a well-ventilated room and wearing a protective mask designed for spray painting. And remember that alcohol has an extremely low flash point and burns with a colorless, almost invisible flame.

Reference Card 16
Large Weeds, Bushes, Tree Foliage, and Twig Textures

(For more information refer to Chapter 6)

Texture	Foliage	Source of Texture
Lichen	Large weeds, bushes, tree foliage	Norwegian lichen sold under Life-Like, Kibri, N.J., Heki, Model Power, Scenic Express, Sun Ray, Woodland Scenics, and Noch labels.Treated with glycerin solution to prevent crumbling. Domestic lichen is available in nearly every forest, from Florida to Maine to the Rockies. Must be treated with glycerin and dye solution on Reference Card 19. Do not use lichen as-is; it is realistic only when covered with traces of ground foam or paper punchings.
Steel wool	Not recommended for model railroads	Slivers can find their way into the magnets of electric motors and cause short circuits. Suitable only for architectural or gaming models. Several grades available in hardware stores.
Rubberized horse hair	Small bushes, twigs	Used as a packing material and for some upholstery. Some plastic scouring pads are similar in texture, such as 3M Scotchbrite and Mr. Potts brand.
Macrame poly-propylene twine	Large weeds, bushes, twigs	From craft supply stores. Color-fast light gray/brown shades suitable as-is for twigs. AMSI and Woodland Scenics Poly Fibers are similar materials.
Woodland Scenics foliage material	Large weeds, bushes, Twigs with foliage, some conifer boughs	Fine-grind foam already glued in place, similar to macramé fiber. Must be pulled apart for the see-through effect of real foliage.
Wool felt	Clumps of tall weeds and small bushes	Individual fibers can be brushed from the felt with a steel- or brass-bristled brush. Use as-is for some weeds or treat with a trace of ground foam.
Air fern	Weeds, bushes, boughs of some conifers	From flower shops and craft supply shops. A live kelly green plant, it requires no treatment, but there is no way to alter the color.
Asparagus fern	Boughs of some, conifers and some weeds	A live fern that must be cut and treated with the glycerin and dye solution on Reference Card 19.
Peat moss	Weeds and some small bushes	From gardening supply and florist shops. Contains enough natural oil to use as-is. Can be spray-painted with latex or acrylic colors.
Caspia, yarrow spirea, and weeds	Weeds, small bushes, deciduous trees, boughs of some conifers	Flowered ends suitable as-is for leaves and pine needles in S or O scale. Must be treated with fine-grind foam for N or HO scales. Dried caspia is available from craft and florist shops.
Peppergrass and candy tuft weeds	Trees, bushes, and large, leafy weeds	From flower shops and craft supply stores. Can be used as-is, but will be more stable if treated with a glycerin solution (Reference Card 19). Can be colored with dye in glycerin solution (see Reference Cards 19 and 17).

Reference Card 17
Weed and Foliage Colors
(For more information refer to Chapter 6)

Color	Polly Scale Paints	Color	Polly Scale Paints
Dark green	1 part CNW Green 414227 1 part water 4 drops detergent per pint	Sage green	5 parts Olive Drab 505224 1 part Dirty White 505205 1 part water 4 drops detergent per pint
Medium green	1 part GN Green 414227 1 part water 4 drops detergent per pint	Straw brown	1 part Mud 414314 1 part water 4 drops detergent per pint
Yellow-Green	9 parts CNWGreen 414227 1 part Mud 4414314 2 parts water 4 drops detergent per pint	Straw yellow	1 part Middlestone 505260 1part ATSF Yellow 414146 2 parts water 4 drops detergent per pint

Directions: Hold the weed or foliage material with tweezers and dip it into the color solution. To apply with an airbrush, thin the mixture with 2 parts water to 1 part paint.

Reference Card 18
Color Dyes for Ground-Foam Foliage
(For more information refer to Chapter 6)

Use conventional fabric dyes sold in grocery and variety stores, such as Rit, Putnam, and Tintex powdered dyes.

Measure the mix dye in hot water exactly as outlined on package. To dye paper punchings, use isopropyl alcohol in place of water. Do not heat the alcohol.

Suggested Colors:

Olive green
Light green
Dark green
Forest green
Jade green
Kelly green
Goldenrod (orange-yellow)
Yellow

When dyeing ground foam or paper punchings, watch for two changes that will occur during the process: (1) the colors will turn several shades lighter as the dyed material dries and (2) each succeeding batch of dyed material will be several shades lighter than the previous batch. After several batches have been dyed, the dye solution will still appear to contain as much color as it did in the beginning, but the material will accept only a trace of the dye. When the dye is exhausted, add another package or two, following the instructions on the package.

If you mix two or more shades of green and/or yellow, use the same brand for all color mixes; do not mix different brands of dye. When the dyed material is dry, store it in Ziploc plastic bags or jars. Label the bags or jars with the date and the colors used so that you can match the colors again.

Reference Card 19
Preserving Solution for Lichen and Other Domestic Moss
(For more information refer to Chapter 6)

For processing a maximum of three gallons of moss (by volume, not weight):

Mix thoroughly:

2 gallons water
1 gallon glycerin
1 package medium green Rit, Putnam, or Tintex powdered dye

Heat mixture to boiling and allow to cool for five minutes.

Submerge the moss in a container and soak it overnight.

Wring out moss by hand. Wear rubber gloves.

Spread moss one layer deep over newspapers and allow to dry completely.

Portions of the moss can be sprayed with or dipped in the Polly Scale colors on Reference Card 17 for variety.

When coloring more than three gallons of moss, use a light, medium, and dark green or yellow dye from Reference Card 17 to match the foliage you are duplicating. Process about one-third of the batch using the formula above. The processing will remove some of the glycerin and most of the dye. To replenish the glycerin, add another quart and another package of dye. Use light green (or yellow) for the first batch, medium green for the second batch, and dark green for the final batch. Each fresh solution must be heated to boiling and cooled for five minutes, and the moss must be allowed to soak overnight.

Reference Card 20
Colors and Techniques for Tree Trunks, Stumps, and Logs

(For more information refer to Chapter 6)

Color/ Techniques	Use	Artist's Acrylics	Polly Scale Paint	Sherwin Williams Interior Latex Paint
Gray-brown	Tree bark	Van Dyke	Roof Brown 414275	1 part Tortoise 1 part Heavy Metal
Red-brown	Tree bark	Burnt Sienna	Boxcar Red 414281	Carob Brown
Gray-white	Tree bark	9 parts White 1 part Burnt Sienna	Dust 414305	1 part Origami White 1 part Tortoise
Shading	All tree bark colors	3 parts Lamp Black 1 part White	Grimy Black 414137	Black Hills
Highlights	All tree bark colors	19 parts White 1 part Burnt Sienna	Aged White 414131	Antique White

Note: Apply with dry-brush technique or as a wash of 9 parts water or denatured alcohol to 1 part mixed paint.

Exposed Wood

Color/ Techniques	Use	Artist's Acrylics	Polly Scale Paint	Sherwin Williams Interior Latex Paint
Fresh cuts	Stumps and log ends	8 parts White 1 part Burnt Sienna 1 part Yellow Ochre	2 parts Aged White 414131 1 part Mud 414314	2 parts Antique White 1 part Luminary Gold
Old cuts	Stumps and log ends	17 parts White 1 part Burnt Sienna 1 part Yellow Ochre 1 part Lamp Black	7 parts Aged White 414131 1 part Grimy Black 414137 2 parts Mud 414314	7 parts Antique White 1 part Tortoise 2 parts Luminary Gold

Note: Apply the shading and highlights for bark to stumps and log ends for a similar effect.

Reference Card 21
Simulated Water
(For more infformation refer to Chapter 8)

Type of Water	**Body of Water**	**Material**
Deep Water Rivers	Lakes Rivers	Two-part Epoxy resins, such as Envirotex or Ultra-Glo. The epoxies usually require an equal mixture of resin and hardener. (Casting resins require a few drops of hardener or catalyst and produce more heat and odor while curing.) Dyes for casting resins, such as those sold by Chemco, can also be used in most epoxy resins to provide a slight blue or blue-green cast.
Shallow water	Streams Ponds	Artist's gloss medium, a clear acrylic-type paint that can be applied thickly enough to form ripples. It dries to a high-gloss finish with little odor.
Rapid water	Rapids Waterfalls Simulated waves in harbors	For deep rapids and harbor scenes, form basic wave shapes with plaster. For shallow rapids, form the bottom of the stream with plaster rocks. For waterfalls, use surgical glass wool, available from wholesale medical supply firms, stringing the wool for vertical waterfall and crumpling it into balls for the foam effect at the base. Coat the wool with several applications of gloss medium, touching the final crests with dabs of pearl-white finger nail polish. Wear rubber gloves when working with the wool.

Reference Card 22
Colors for Epoxy Water
For more information refer to Chapter 8)

Color	Use	Formula
Blue-green	Mountain streams Rivers	1 drop blue resin dye 1 drop green resin dye 4 ounces epoxy Mix thoroughly while blending resin and hardener.
Blue	Deep lakes Harbors	12 drops blue resin dye 4 ounces epoxy Mix thoroughly while blending resin and hardener.
Gray-green	Harbors Oceans Deep rivers Lakes and ponds	1 drop green resin dye 1 drop black resin dye 8 ounces epoxy Mix thoroughly while blending resin and hardener.
Brown	Flooded rivers Shallow streams Ponds	1 drop brown resin dye 4 ounces epoxy Mix thoroughly while blending resin and hardener.
White	Crests of waves Waterfalls Rapids Breakers	1 part white acrylic 2 parts gloss medium Paint and allow to dry thoroughly. Apply small dabs of pearl-white fingernail polish to crests of waves and foam.

Note: To achieve the "wet" look, apply at least 1/32 inch of epoxy or a thick layer of gloss medium over the final layer of colored resin. Work small waves into epoxy during the last few minutes of hardening.

Reference Card 23
Three-Step Skin-Tone Painting
(For more information refer to Chapter 9)

	Polly Scale Paint
1. Paint all flesh areas with basic skin tone	1 part Flesh 505212 1 part Reefer White 414113
2. Brush on overall wash of shadow color to fill in hollows and creases in skin areas	1 part Earth Brown 5050240 19 parts water 4 drops dishwashing detergent per pint
3. Dry-brush highlights, such as cheeks, forehead, chin, backs of fingers, and wrists	1 part Flesh 505212 or 1 part Mud 414314 9 parts water 4 drops dishwashing detergent per pint